HISTORY OF RICHARD III

Thomas More

Originally Published by: Richard Grafton
Edited by: D.P. Curtin

Dalcassian
Publishing
Company
PHILADELPHIA, PA

Library of Congress Cataloging-in-Publication Data

Copyright © 2019 Dalcassian Publishing Co.
In association with St. Macartan Press
All rights reserved.

The History of King Richard the Third (Unfinished) By Thomas More

King Edward of that name the fourth, after that he had lived fifty and three years, seven months, and five days, and thereof reigned two and twenty years, one month, and eight days, died at Westminster the ninth day of April, the year of or redemption, a thousand four hundred four score and three, leaving much fair issue, that is to wit, Edward the Prince, thirteen year of age: Richard Duke of York, two year younger: Elizabeth, whose fortune and grace was after to be Queen, wife unto King Henry the seventh, and mother unto the eighth: Cecily not so fortunate as fair: Brigette, which representing the virtue of her, whose name she bore, professed and observed a religious life in Dartford, an house of close Nuns: Anne, that was after honourably married unto Thomas, then Lord Howard, and after Earl of Surrey. And Katheryne which long time tossed in either fortune sometime in wealth, oft in adversity, at the last, if this be the last, for yet she liveth, is by the benignity of her Nephew, King Henry the eighth, in very prosperous estate, and worthy her birth and virtue.

This noble Prince deceased at his Palace of Westminster, and with great funeral honour and heaviness of his people from thence conveyed, was entered at Windsor. A King of such governance and behaviour in time of peace (for in war each party must needs be other's enemy) that there was never any Prince of this land attaining the Crown by battle, so heartily beloved with the substance of the people: nor he himself so specially in any part of his life, as at the time of his death. Which favour and affection yet after his decease, by the cruelty, mischief, and trouble of the tempestuous world that followed, highly toward him more increased. At such time as he died, the displeasure of those that bore him grudge, for King Henry's sake the sixth, whom he deposed, was well assuaged, and in effect quenched, in that that many of them were dead in more than twenty years of his reign, a great part of a long life. And many of them in the mean season grown into his favour, of which he was never strange.

He was a goodly personage, and very princely to behold, of heart courageous, politic in council, in adversity nothing abashed, in prosperity, rather joyful than proud, in peace just and merciful, in war, sharp and fierce, in the field, bold and hardy, and natheless no farther than wisdom would, adventurous. Whose wars who so well consider, he shall no less commend his wisdom where he voided, than his manhood where he vanquished. He was of visage lovely, of body mighty, strong, and clean made: Howbeit in his latter days with over liberal diet, somewhat corpulent and boorly, and natheless not uncomely, he was of youth greatly given to fleshly wantonness: from which health of body in great prosperity and fortune, without a special grace hardly refraineth. This fault not greatly grieved the people: for neither could any one man's pleasure, stretch and extend to the displeasure of very many, and was without violence, and over that in his latter days: blessed and well loved. In which time of his latter days, this Realm was in quiet and prosperous estate: no fear of outward enemies, no war in hand, nor none toward, but such as no man looked for: the people toward the Prince, not in a constrained fear, but in a willing and loving obedience: among themselves, the commons in good peace. The Lords whom he knew at variance, himself in his death bed appeased. He had left all gathering of money (which is the only thing that withdraweth the hearts of Englishmen from the Prince) nor any thing intendeth he to take in hand, by which he should be driven thereto, for his tribute out of France he had before obtained. And the year foregoing his death, he had obtained Berwick. And albeit that all the time of his reign, he was with his people, so benign, courteous and so familiar, that no part of his virtues was more esteemed: yet that condition in the end of his days (in which many princes by a long continued sovereignty, decline in to a proud port from debonair behaviour of their beginning) marvellously in him grew and increased: so far forth that in the Summer the last that ever he saw, his highness being at Windsor in hunting, sent for the Mayor and Aldermen of London to him, for none other errand, but to have them hunt and be merry with him, where he made them not so straitly, but so friendly and so familiar cheer, and sent venison from thence so freely into the City, that no one thing in many days before, gave him either more hearts or more hearty favour among the common people, which oftentimes more esteem and take for greater kindness, a little courtesy, than a great benefit. So deceased (as I have said) this noble King, in that time, in which his life was most desired. Whose love of his people and their entire affection toward him, had been to his noble children (having in themselves also as many gifts of nature, as many Princely virtues, as much goodly towardness as their age could receive) a marvellous fortress and sure armour, if division and dissension of their friends, had not unarmed them, and left them destitute, and the execrable desire of sovereignty, provoked him to their destruction, which if either kind or kindness had holden place, must needs have been their chief defence. For Richard the Duke of Gloucester, by nature their Uncle, by office their Protector, to their father beholden, to themselves by oath and allegiance bound, all the bands broken that bind man and man together, without any respect of God or the world, unnaturally contrived to bereave them, not only their dignity, but also their lives. But forasmuch as this Duke's demeanour ministreth in effect all the whole matter whereof this book shall entreat, it is therefore convenient, somewhat to show you ere we farther go, what manner of man this was, that could find in his heart, so much mischief to conceive.

Richard Duke of York, a noble man and a mighty, began not by war, but by law, to challenge the crown, putting his claim into the parliament. Where his cause was either for right or favour so farforth advanced, that King Henry his blood (albeit he had a goodly Prince) utterly rejected, the Crown was by authority of parliament entailed unto the Duke of York and his issue male in remainder immediately after the death of King Henry. But the Duke not enduring so long to tarry, but intending under pretext of dissension and debate arising in the realm, to prevent his time, and take upon him the rule in King Harry his life, was with many nobles of the realm at Wakefield slain, leaving three sons, Edward, George, and Richard. All three as they were great states of birth, so were they great and stately of stomach, greedy and ambitious of authority, and impatient of partners. Edward revenging his father's death, deprived King Henry, and attained the crown. George Duke of Clarence was a goodly noble Prince, and at all points fortunate, if either his own ambition had not set him against his brother, or the envy of his enemies, his brother against him. For were it by the Queen and the Lords of her blood which highly maligned the King's kindred (as women commonly not of malice but of nature hate them whom their husbands love) or were it a proud appetite of the

Duke himself intending to be King: at the lest wise heinous Treason was there laid to his charge, and finally were he faulty, were he faultless, attainted was he by parliament, and judged to the death, and thereupon hastily drowned in a butt of Malmsey, whose death King Edward (albeit he commanded it) when he wist it was done, piteously bewailed and sorrowfully repented.

Richard the third son, of whom we now entreat, was in wit and courage equal with either of them, in body and prowess far under them both, little of stature, ill featured of limbs, crook-backed, his left should much higher than his right, hard favoured of visage, and such as is in states called warly, in other men otherwise, he was malicious, wrathful, envious, and from afore his birth, ever froward. It is for truth reported, that the Duchess his mother had so much ado in her travail, that she could not be delivered of him uncut: and that he came into the world with the feet forward, as men be born outward, and (as the fame runneth) also not untoothed, whither men of hatred report above the truth, or else that nature changed her course in his beginning, which in the course of his life many things unnaturally committed. None evil captain was he in the war, as to which his disposition was more meetly than for peace. Sundry victories had he, and sometime overthrows, but never in default as for his own person, either of hardiness or politic order, free was he called of dispense, and somewhat above his power liberal, with large gifts he got him unsteadfast friendship, for which he was fain to pill and spoil in other places, and get him steadfast hatred. He was close and secret, a deep dissimuler, lowly of countenance, arrogant of heart, outwardly companionable where he inwardly hated, not letting to kiss whom he thought to kill: dispitous and cruel, not for evil will always, but after for ambition, and either for the surety or increase of his estate. Friend and foe was much what indifferent, where his advantage grew, he spared no man death, whose life withstood his purpose. He slew with his own hands King Henry the sixth, being prisoner in the Tower, as men constantly say, and that without commandment or knowledge of the King, which would undoubtedly if he had intended that thing, have appointed that butcherly office, to some other than his own born brother.

Some wise men also ween, that his drift covertly conveyed, lacked not in helping forth his brother of Clarence to his death: which he resisted openly, howbeit somewhat (as men deemed) more faintly than he that were heartily minded to his wealth. And they that thus deem, think that he long time in King Edward's life, forethought to be King in case that that King his brother (whose life he looked that evil diet should shorten) should happen to decease (as in deed he did) while his children were young. And they deem, that for this intent he was glad of his brother's death that Duke of Clarence, whose life must needs have hindered him so intending, whither the same Duke of Clarence had he kept him true to his nephew the young King, or enterprised to be King himself. But of all this Pointe, is there no certainty, and whoso divineth upon conjectures, may as well shoot to far as to short. Howbeit this have I by credible information learned, that the self night in which King Edward died, one Mistlebrooke long ere morning, came in great haste to the house of one Pottier dwelling in Redcross Street without Cripplegate: and when he was with hasty rapping quickly let in, he showed unto Pottier that King Edward was departed. By my truth man quod Pottier then will my master the Duke of Gloucester be King. What cause he had so to think hard it is to say, whether he being toward him, any thing knew that he such thing purposed, or otherwise had any inkling thereof: for he was not likely to speak it of nought.

But now to return to the course of this history, were it that the Duke of Gloucester had of old foreminded this conclusion, or was now at erst thereunto moved, and put in hope by the occasion of the tender age of the young Princes, his Nephews (as opportunity and likelihood of speed, putteth a man in courage of that he never intended) certain is it that he contrived their destruction, with the usurpation of the regal dignity upon himself. And for as much as he well wist and helped to maintain, a long continued grudge and heart burning between the Queen's kindred and the King's blood either party envying other's authority, he now thought that their division should be (as it was in deed) a fortherly beginning to the pursuit of his intent, and a sure ground for the foundation of all his building if he might first under the pretext of revenging of old displeasure, abuse the anger and ignorance of the one party, to the destruction of the other: and then win to his purpose as many as he could: and those that could not be won, might be lost ere they looked therefore. For of one thing was he certain, that if his intent were perceived, he should soon have made peace between the both parties, with his own blood.

King Edward in his life, albeit that this dissension between his friends somewhat irked him: yet in his good health he somewhat the less regarded it, because he thought whatsoever business should fall between them, himself should always be able to rule both the parties.

But in his last sickness, when he received his natural strengthen so far enfeebled, that he despaired all recovery, then he considering the youth of his children, albeit he nothing less mistrusted than that that happened, yet well foreseeing that many harms might grow by their debate, while the youth of his children should lack discretion of themselves and good council, of their friends, of which either party should council for their own commodity and rather by pleasant advice to win themselves favour, than by profitable advertisement to do the children good, he called some of them before him that were at variance, and in especial the Lord Marquis Dorset the Queen's son by her first husband, and Richard the Lord Hastings, a noble man, then Lord Chamberlain against whom the Queen specially grudged, for that great favour the King bore him, and also for that she thought him secretly familiar with the King in wanton company. Her kindred also bore him sore, as well for that the King had made him captain of Calais (which office the Lord Rivers, brother to the Queen claimed of the King's former promise as for divers other great gifts which he received, that they looked for.

When these Lords with divers other of both the parties were come in presence, the King lifting up himself and underset with pillows, as it is reported on this wise said unto them. My Lords, my dear kinsmen and allies, in what plight I lie you see, and I feel. By which the less while I look to live with you, the more deeply am I moved to care in what case I leave you, for such as I leave you, such be my children like to find you. Which if they should (that God forbid) find you at variance, might hap to fall themselves at war ere their discretion would serve to set you at peace. Ye see their youth, of which I reckon the only surety to rest in your concord. For it sufficeth not that all you love them, if each of you hate other. If they were men, your faithfulness haply would suffice. But childhood must be maintained by men's authority, and slipper youth underpropped with elder council, which neither they can have, but ye give it, nor ye give it, if ye agree not. For where each laboureth to break that the other maketh, and for hated of each other's person, impugneth each other's council, there must it needs be long ere any good conclusion go forward. And also while either party laboureth to be chief, flattery shall have more place than plain and faithful advice, of which must needs ensue the evil bringing up of the Prince, whose mind in tender youth infect, shall readily fall to mischief and riot, and draw down with this noble realm to ruin, but if grace turn him to wisdom: which if God send, then they that by evil means before pleased him best, shall after fall farthest out of favour, so that ever at length evil drifts draw to nought, and good plain ways prosper. Great variance hath there long been between you, not always for great causes. Some time a thing right well intended, our misconstruction turneth unto worse or a small displeasure done us, either our own affection or evil tongues aggrieveth. But this wot I well ye never had so great cause of hatred, as ye have of love. That we be all men, that we be Christian men, this shall I leave for preachers to tell you (and yet I wot ne'er whither any preacher's words ought more to move you, than his that is by and by going to the place that they all preach of.) But this that I desire you to remember, that the one part of you is of my blood, the other of mine allies, and each of you with other, either of kindred or affinity, which spiritual kindred of affinity, if the sacraments of Christ's Church, bear that weight with us that would God they did, should no less move us to charity, than the respected of fleshly consanguinity. Our Lord forbid, that you love together the worse, for the self cause that you ought to love the better. And yet that happeneth. And no where find we so deadly debate, as among them, which by nature and law most ought to agree together. Such a pestilent serpent is ambition and desire of vainglory and sovereignty, which among states where he once entereth creepeth forth so far, till with division and variance he turneth all to mischief. First longing to be next the best, afterwards equal with the best, and at last chief and above the best. Of which immoderate appetite of worship, and thereby of debate and dissension what loss what sorrow, what trouble hath within these few years grown in this realm, I pray God as well forget as we well remember.

Which things if I could as well have foreseen, as I have with my more pain than pleasure proved, by God's blessed Lady (that was ever his oath) I would never have won the courtesy of men's knees, with the loss of so many heads. But sithen things passed cannot be again called, much ought we the more beware, by what occasion we have taken so great hurt afore, that we eftesoon fall not in that occasion again. Now be those griefs passed, and all is (God be thanked) quiet, and likely right well to prosper in wealthful peace under your cousins my children, if God send them life and you love. Of which two things, the less loss were they by whom though God did his pleasure, yet should the Realm always find King's and peradventure as good King's. But if you among yourselves in a child's reign fall at debate, many a good man shall perish and haply he too, and ye too, ere this land find peace again. Wherefore in these last words that ever I look to speak with you: I exhort you and require you all, for the love that I have ever born to you, for the love that our Lord beareth to us all, from this time forward, all griefs forgotten, each of you love other. Which I verily trust you will, if ye any thing earthly regard, either God or your King, affinity or kindred, this realm, your own country, or your own surety. And therewithal the King no longer enduring to sit up, laid him down on his right side, his face toward them: and none was there present that could refrain from weeping. But the Lords recomforting him with as good words as they could, and answering for the time as they thought to stand with his pleasure, there in his presence (as by their words appeared each forgave other, and joined their hands together, when (as it after appeared by their deeds) their hearts, were far asunder.

As soon as the King was departed, that noble prince his son drew toward London, which at the time of his decease, kept his household at Ludlow in Wales. Which country being far off from the law and recourse to justice, was begun to be far out of good will and waxen wild, robbers and rievers walking at liberty uncorrected. And for this encheason the prince was in the life of his father sent thither, to the end that the authority of his presence, should refrain evil disposed persons from the boldness of their former outrages, to the governance and ordering of this young prince at his sending thither, was there appointed Sir Antony Wodvile Lord Rivers and brother unto the Queen, a right honourable man, as valiant of hand as politic in council. Adjoined were there unto him other of the same party, and in effect every one as he was nearest of kin unto the Queen, so was planted next about the prince. That drift by the Queen not unwisely devised, whereby her blood might of youth be rooted in the prince's favour, the Duke of Gloucester turned unto their destruction, and upon that ground set the foundation of all his unhappy building. For whomsoever he perceived, either at variance with them, or bearing himself their favour, he broke unto them, some by mouth, some by writing and secret messengers, that it neither was reason nor in any wise to be suffered, that the young King their master and kinsman, should be in the hands and custody of his mother's kindred, sequestered in manner from their company and attendance, of which every one ought him as faithful service as they, and many of them far more honourable part of kin than his mother's side: whose blood (quod he) saving the King's pleasure, was full unmeetly to be matched with his: which now to be as who say removed from the King, and the less noble to be left about him, is (quod he) neither honourable to his majesty, nor unto us, and also to his grace no surety to have the mightiest of his friends from him, and unto us no little jeopardy, to suffer our well proved evil willers, to grow in overgreat authority with the prince in youth, namely which is light of belief and soon persuaded. Ye remember I trow King Edward himself, albeit he was a man of age and of discretion, yet was he in many things ruled by the bend, more than stood either with his honour, or our profit, or with the commodity of any man else, except only the immoderate advancement of themselves. Which whither they sorer thirsted after their own weal, or our woe, it were hard I ween to guess. And if some folk's friendship had not holden better place with the King, than any respect of kindred, they might peradventure easily have been trapped and brought to confusion some of us ere this. Why not as easily as they have done some other already, as near of his royal blood as we. But our Lord hath wrought his will, and thank be to his grace that peril is past. Howbeit as great is growing, if we suffer this young King in our enemies' hand, which without his witting, might abuse the name of his commandment, to any of our undoing, which thing God and good provision forbid. Of which good provision none of us hath any thing the less need, for the late made atonement, in which the King's pleasure had more place than the parties' wills. Nor none of us I believe is so unwise, oversoon to trust a new friend made of an old foe, or to think that an hourly kindness, suddenly contract in one hour, continued yet scant a fortnight, should be deeper settled in their stomachs: than a long accustomed malice many years rooted.

With these words and writings and such other, the Duke of Gloucester soon set afire, them that were of themselves ethe to kindle, and in special twain, Edward Duke of Buckingham, and Richard Lord Hastings and Chamberlain, both men of honour and of great power. The one by long succession from his ancestry, the other by his office and the King's favour. These two not bearing each to other so much love, as hatred both unto the Queen's part: in this point accorded together with the Duke of Gloucester, that they would utterly amove from the King's company, all his mother's friends, under the name of their enemies. Upon this concluded, the Duke of Gloucester understanding, that the Lords which at that time were about the King, intended to bring him up to his Coronation, accompanied with such power of their friends, that it should be hard for him to bring his purpose to pass, without the gathering and great assemble of people and in manner of open war, whereof the end he wist was doubtuous, and in which the King being on their side, his part should have the face and name of a rebellion: he secretly therefore by divers means, caused the Queen to be persuaded, and brought in the mind, that it neither were need, and also should be jeopardous, the King to come up strong. For where as now every Lord loved other, and none other thing studied upon, but about the Coronation and honour of the King: if the Lords of her kindred should assemble in the King's name much people, they should give the Lords atwixt whom and them had been sometime debate, to fear and suspect, lest they should gather this people, not for the King's safeguard whom no man impugned, but for their destruction, having more regard to their old variance, than their new atonement. For which cause they should assemble on the other party much people against for their defence, whose power she wist well far stretched. And thus should all the realm fall on a roar. And of all the hurt that thereof should ensue, which was likely not to be little, and the most harm there like to fall where she least would, all the world would put her and her kindred in the weight, and say that they had unwisely and untruly also, broken the amity and peace that the King her husband so prudently made, between his kin and hers in his death bed, and which the other party faithfully observed.

The Queen being in this wise persuaded, such word sent unto her son, and unto her brother being about the King, and over that the Duke of Gloucester himself and other Lords the chief of his band, wrote unto the King so reverently, and to the Queen's friends, there so lovingly, that they nothing Earthly mistrusting, brought the King up in great haste, not in good speed, with a sober company. Now was the King in his way to London gone, from Northampton, when these Dukes of Gloucester and Buckingham came thither. Where remained behind, the Lord Rivers the King's uncle, intending on the morrow to follow the King, and be with him at Stony Stratford eleven miles thence, early ere he departed. So was there made that night much friendly cheer between these Dukes and the Lord Rivers a great while. But incontinent after that they were openly with great courtesy departed, and the Lord Rivers lodged, the Dukes secretly with a few of their most privy friends, set them down in council, wherein they spent a great part of the night. And at their rising in the dawning of the day, they sent about privily to their servants in their inns and lodgings about, giving the commandment to make themselves shortly ready, for their Lords were to horsebackward. Upon which messages, many of their folk were attendant, when many of the Lord River's servants were unready. Now had these Dukes taken also into their custody the keys of the inn, that none should pass forth without their licence. And over this in the high way toward Stony Stratford where the King lay, they had bestowed certain of their folk, that should send back again, and compel to return, any man that were gotten out of Northampton toward Stony Stratford, till they should give other licence. For as much as the Dukes themselves intended for the show of their diligence, to be the first that should that day attend upon the King's highness out of that town: thus bore they folk in hand. But when the Lord Rivers understood the gates closed, and the ways on every side beset, neither his servants nor himself suffered to go out, perceiving well so great a thing without his knowledge not begun for nought, comparing this manner present with this last night's cheer, in so few hours so great a change marvellously misliked. How be it sith he could not get away, and keep himself close, he would not, lest he should seem to hide himself for some secret fear of his own fault, whereof he saw no such cause in himself: he determined upon the surety of his own conscience, to go boldly to them, and inquire what this matter might mean. Whom as soon as they saw, they began to quarrel with him, and say, that he intended to set distance between the King and them, and to bring them to confusion, but it should not lie in his power. And when he began (as he was a very well spoken man,) in goodly wise to excuse himself, they tarried not the end of his answer, but shortly took him and put him in ward, and that done, forthwith went to horseback, and took the way to Stony Stratford. Where they found the King with his company ready to leap on horseback, and depart forward, to leave that lodging for them, because it was too strait for both companies. And as soon as they came in his presence, they light down with all their company about them. To whom the Duke of Buckingham said, go afore Gentlemen and yeomen, keep your rooms. And thus in a goodly array, they came to the King, and on their knees in very humble wise, salved his grace: which received them in very joyous and amiable manner, nothing earthly knowing nor mistrusting as yet. But even by and by in his presence, they picked a quarrel to the Lord Richard Gray, the King's other brother by his mother, saying that he with the Lord Marquis his brother and the Lord Rivers his uncle, had compassed to rule the King and the realm, and to set variance among the states, and to subdue and destroy the noble blood of the realm. Toward the accomplishing whereof, they said that the Lord Marquis had entered into the Tower of London, and thence taken out the King's Treasure, and sent men to the sea. All which thing these Dukes wist well were done for good purposes and necessary by the whole council at London, saving that somewhat they must say. Unto which words, the King answered, what my brother Marquis hath done I cannot say. But in good faith I dare well answer for mine uncle Rivers and my brother here, that they be innocent of any such matters. Yea my liege quod the Duke of Buckingham they have kept their dealing in these matters far from the knowledge of your good grace. And forthwith they arrested the Lord Richard and Sir Thomas Vaughan knighte, in the King's presence, and brought the King and all back unto Northampton, where they took again further council. And there they sent away from the King whom it pleased them, and set new servants about him, such as liked them better than him. At which dealing he wept and was nothing content, but it booted not. And at dinner the Duke of Gloucester sent a dish from his own table to the Lord Rivers, praying him to be of good cheer, all should be well enough. And he thanked the Duke, and prayed the messenger to bear it to his nephew the Lord Richard with the same message for his comfort, who he thought had more need of comfort, as one to whom such adversity was strange. But himself had been all his days in ure therewith, and therefore could bear it the better. But for all this comfortable courtesy of the Duke of Gloucester he sent the Lord

Rivers and the Lord Richard with Sir Thomas Vaughan into the North country into divers places to prison, and afterward all to Pontefract, where they were in conclusion beheaded.

In this wise the Duke of Gloucester took upon himself the order and governance of the young King, whom with much honour and humble reverence he conveyed upward toward the city. But anon the tidings of this matter came hastily to the Queen, a little before the midnight following, and that in the sorest wise that the King her son was taken, her brother, her son and her other friends arrested, and sent no man wist whither, to be done with God wot what. With which tidings the Queen in great fright and heaviness, bewailing her child's ruin, her friends' mischance, and her own infortune, damning the time that ever she dissuaded the gathering of power about the King, got herself in all the haste possible with her younger son and her daughters out of the Palace of Westminster in which she then lay, into the Sanctuary, lodging herself and her company there in the Abbot's place.

Now came there in one likewise not long after midnight, from the Lord Chamberlain unto the archbishop of York then Chancellor of England to his place not far from Westminster. And for that he showed his servants that he had tidings of so great importance, that his master gave him in charge, not to forbear his rest, they letted not to wake him, nor he to admit this messenger in to his bed side. Of whom he heard, that these Dukes were gone back with the King's grace from Stony Stratford unto Northampton. Notwithstanding Sir quod he, my Lord sendeth your Lordship word, that there is no fear. For he assureth you that all shall be well. I assure him quod the Archbishop be it as well as it will, it will never be so well as we have seen it. And thereupon by and by after the messenger departed, he caused in all the haste all his servants to be called up, and so with his own household about him, and every man weaponed, he took the great Seal with him, and came yet before day unto the Queen. About whom he found much heaviness, rumble, haste and business, carriage and conveyance of her stuff into Sanctuary, chests, coffers, packs, fardels, trusses, all on men's backs, no man unoccupied; some lading, some going, some discharging, some coming for more, some breaking down the walls to bring in the next way, and some yet drew to them that holpe to carry a wronged way. The Queen herself sat alone alow on the rushes all desolate and dismayed, whom the Archbishop comforted in the best manner he could, showing her that he trusted the matter was nothing so sore as she took it for. And that he was put in good hope and out of fear, by the message sent him from the Lord Chamberlain. Ah woe worth him, quod she, for he is one of them that laboureth to destroy me and my blood. Madame quod he, be ye of good cheer. For I assure you if they crown any other King than your son, whom they now have with them, we shall on the morrow crown his brother whom you have here with you. And here is the great Seal, which in likewise as that noble prince your husband delivered it unto me, so here I deliver it unto you, to the use and behoof of your son, and therewith he betook her the great Seal, and departed home again, yet in the dawning of the day. By which time he might in his chamber window, see all the Thames full of boats of the Duke of Gloucester's servants, watching that no man should go to Sanctuary, nor none could pass unsearched. Then was there great commotion and murmur as well in other places about, as specially in the city, the people diversely divining upon this dealing. And some Lords, Knights, and Gentlemen either for favour of the Queen, or for fear of themselves, assembled in sundry companies, and went flockmeal in harness: and many also, for that they reckoned this demeanour attempted, not so specially against the other Lords, as against the King himself in the disturbance of his Coronation. But then by and by the Lords assembled together at London. Toward which meeting, the Archbishop of York fearing that it would be ascribed (as it was in deed) to his overmuch lightness, that he had so suddenly had yielded up the great seal to the Queen, to whom the custody thereof nothing pertained, without especial commandment, of the King, secretly sent for the Seal again, and brought it with him after the customable manner. And at this meeting, the Lord Hastings, whose truth toward the King no man doubted nor needed to doubt, persuaded the Lords to believe, that the Duke of Gloucester, was sure and fastly faithful to his prince, and that the Lord Rivers and Lord Richard with the other knights were for matters attempted by them against the Dukes of Gloucester and Buckingham, put under arrest for their surety, not for the King's jeopardy: and that they were also in safeguard, and there no longer should remain, than till the matter were, not by the Dukes only, but also by all the other Lords of the King's council indifferently examined, and by other discretions ordered, and either judged or appeased. But one thing he advised them beware, that they judged not the matter to farforth, ere they knew the truth, nor turning their private grudges into the common hurt, irritating and provoking men unto anger, and disturbing the King's Coronation, toward which the Dukes were coming up, that they might peradventure bring the matter so far out of joint, that it should never be brought in frame again. Which strife if it should hap as it were likely to come to a field, though both parties were in all things equal, yet should the authority be on that side where the King is himself. With these persuasions of the Lord Hastings, whereof part himself believed, of part he wist the contrary, these commotions were somewhat appeased. But specially, by that that the Dukes of Gloucester and Buckingham were so near, and came so shortly on with the King, in none other manner, with none other voice or semblance, than to his coronation, causing the fame to be blown about, that these Lords and knights which were taken, had contrived the destruction of the Dukes of Gloucester and Buckingham, and of other the noble blood of the Realm, to the end that themselves would alone, demean and govern the King at their pleasure. And for the colourable proof thereof, such of the Duke's servants as rode with the carts of their stuff that were taken (among which stuff no marvel though some were harness, which at the breaking up of that household, must needs either be brought away or cast away) they showed unto the people all the way as they went: lo here be the barrels of harness that this traitors had privily conveyed in their carriage to destroy the noble Lords with all. This devise all be it that it made the matter to wise men more unlikely, well perceiving that the intenders of such a purpose, would rather have had their harness on the backs, than to have bound them up in barrels, yet much part of the common people were therewith very well satisfied, and said it were alms to hang them.

When the King approached near to the city, Edmond Shaw goldsmith then Mayor, with William White and John Mathew sheriff, and all the other aldermen in scarlet with five hundred horse of the citizens in violet, received him reverently at Harnesy: and riding from thence, accompanied him in to the city, which he entered the fourth day of May, the first and last year of his reign. But the Duke of Gloucester bore him in open sight so reverently to the Prince, with all semblance of lowliness, that from the great obloquy in which he was so late before, he was suddenly fallen in so great trust, that at the council next assembled, he was made the only man chose and thought most meet, to be Protector of the King and his realm, so (that were it destiny or were it folly) the lamb was betaken to the wolf to keep. At which council also the Archbishop of York Chancellor of England, which had delivered up the great Seal to the Queen, was thereof greatly reproved, and the Seal taken from him and delivered to doctor Russell, bishop of Lincoln, a wise man and a good and of much experience, and one of the best learned men undoubtedly that England had in his time. Divers Lords and knights were appointed unto divers rooms. The Lord Chamberlain and some other, kept still their offices that they had before. Now all were it so that the Protector so sore thirsted for the finishing of that he had begun, that thought every day a year till it were achieved, yet durst he no further attempt as long as had but half his prey in his hand: well witting that if he deposed the one brother, all the Realm would fall to the other, if he either remained in Sanctuary, or should haply be shortly conveyed to his farther liberty. Wherefore incontinent at the next meeting of the Lords at the council, he proposed unto them, that it was a heinous deed of the Queen, and proceeding of great malice toward the King's councillors, that she should keep in Sanctuary the King's brother from him, whose special pleasure and comfort were to have his brother with him. And that by her done to none other intent, but to bring all the Lords in obloquy and murmur of the people. As though they were not to be trusted with the King's brother, that by the assent of the nobles of the land were appointed as the King's nearest friends, to the tuition of his own royal person. The prosperity whereof standeth (quod he) not all in keeping from enemies or ill viand, but partly also in recreation and moderate pleasure: which he cannot in this tender youth take in the company of ancient persons, but in the familiar conversation of those that be neither far under, nor far above his age. And nathless of estate convenient to accompany his noble majesty. Wherefore with whom rather than with his own brother? And if any man think this consideration light (Which I think no man thinketh that loveth the King) let him consider that sometime without small things greater cannot stand. And verily it redoundeth greatly to the dishonour both of the King's highness and of all us that been about his grace, to have it run in every man's mouth, not in this realm only, but also in other lands (as evil words walk far:) that the King's brother should be fain to keep Sanctuary. For every man will ween, that no man will so do for nought. And such evil opinion once fastened in men's hearts, hard it is to wrest out, and may grow to more grief than any man here can divine.

Wherefore me thinketh it were not worst to send unto the Queen for the redress of this matter, some honourable trusty man, such as both tendereth the King's weal, and the honour of his council, and is also in favour and credence with her. For all which considerations, none seemeth me more meetly than our reverent father here present, my Lord Cardinal, who may in this matter do most good of any man, if it please him to take the pain. Which I doubt not of his goodness he will not refuse, for the King's sake and ours, and wealth of the young Duke himself the King's most honourable brother, and after my sovereign Lord himself, my most dear Nephew: considered that thereby shall be ceased the slanderous rumour and obloquy now going and the hurts avoided that thereof might ensue, and much rest and quiet grow to all the realm. And if she be percase so obstinate, and so precisely set upon her own will, that neither his wise and faithful advertisement can move her, nor any man's reason content her: then shall we by mine advice, by the King's authority fetch him out of that prison, and bring him to his noble presence, in whose continual company he shall be so well cherished and so honourably entreated, that all the world shall to our honour and her reproach, perceive that it was only malice, frowardeness, or folly, that caused her to keep him there. This is my mind in this matter for this time, except any of your Lordships any thing perceive to the contrary. For never shall I by God's grace so wed myself to mine own will, but that I shall be ready to change it upon your better advices.

When the Protector had said, all the council affirmed that the motion was good and reasonable, and to the King and the Duke his brother, honourable, and a thing that should cease great murmur in the realm, if the mother might be by good means induced to deliver him. Which thing the Archbishop of York, whom they all agreed also to be thereto most convenient, took upon him to move her, and therein to do his uttermost devoir.

Howbeit if she could be in no wise entreated with her good will to deliver him, then thought he and such other as were of the spirituality present, that it were not in any wise to be attempted to take him out against her will. For it would be a thing that should turn to the great grudge of all men, and high displeasure of God, if the privilege of the holy place should now be broken?

Which had so many years been kept, which both Kings and Popes so good had granted, so many had confirmed, and which holy ground was more than five hundred year ago by Saint Peter his own person in spirit, accompanied with great multitude of Angels, by night so specially hallowed and dedicate to God, (for the proof whereof they have yet in the Abbey Saint Peters cope to show) that from that time hitherward, was there never so undevout a King, that durst that sacred place violate, or so holy a Bishop that durst it presume to consecrate. And therefore (quod the Archbishop of York) God forbid that any man should for any thing earthly enterprise to break the immunity, and liberty of that sacred Sanctuary, that hath been the safeguard of so many a good man's life. And I trust (quod he) with God's grace, we shall not need it. But for any manner need, I would not we should do it. I trust that she shall be with reason contented, and all thing in good manner obtained. And if it happen that I bring it not so to pass, yet shall I toward it so farforth do my best, that ye shall all well perceive, that no lack of my devoir, but the mother's dread and womanish fear, shall be the let. Womanish fear, nay womanish frowardness (quod the Duke of Buckingham.) For I dare take it upon my soul, she well knoweth she needeth no such thing to fear, either for her son or for herself. For as for her, here is no man that will be at war with women. Would God some of the men of her kin, were women too, and then should all be soon in rest. Howbeit there is none of her kin the less loved, for that they be her kin, but for their own evil deserving. And natheless if we loved neither her nor her kin, yet were there no cause to think that we should hate the King's noble brother, to whose Grace we ourselves be of kin. Whose honour if she as much desired as our dishonour, and as much regard took to his wealth, as to her own will, she would be as loath to suffer him from the King, as any of us be. For if she have any wit, (as would God she had as good will as she hath shrewd wit) she reckoneth herself no wiser than she thinketh some that be here, of whose faithful mind, she nothing doubteth, but verily believeth and knoweth, that they would be as sorry of his harm as herself, and yet would have him from her if she bide there. And we all

(I think) content, that both be with her, if she come thence and bide in such place where they may with their honour be.

Now then if she refuse in the deliverance of him, to follow the council of them whose wisdom she knoweth, whose truth she well trusteth: it is ethe to perceive, that frowardness letteth her, and not fear. But go to suppose that she fear (as who may let her to fear her own shadow) the more she feareth to deliver him, the more ought we fear to leave him in her hands . For if she caste such fond doubts, that she fear his hurt: then will she fear that he shall be fetched thence. For she will soon think, that if men were set (Which God forbid) upon so great a mischief, the sanctuary would little let them. Which good men might as me thinketh without sin somewhat less regard than they do.

Now then if she doubt lest he might be fetched from her, is it not likely enough that she shall send him somewhere out of the realm? Verily I look for none other. And I doubt not but she now as sore mindeth it, as we the let thereof. And if she might happen to bring that to pass, (as it were no great mastery, we letting her alone) all the world would say that we were a wise sort of councillors about a King, that let his brother be cast away under our noses. And therefore I ensure you faithfully for my mind, I will rather maugre her mind, fetch him away, than leave him there, till her frowardness or fond fear convey him away. And yet will I break no Sanctuary therefore. For verily sith the privileges of that place and other like, have been of long continued, I am not he that would be about to break them. And in good faith if they were now to begin, I would not be he that should be about to make them. Yet will I not say nay, but that it is a deed of pity, that such men as the sea or their evil debtors have brought in poverty, should have some place of liberty, to keep their bodies out of the danger of their cruel creditors. And also if the Crown happen (as it hath done) to come in question, while either part taketh other as traitors, I will well there be some places of refuge for both. But as for thieves, of which these places be full, and which never fall from the craft, after they once fall thereto, it is pity the sanctuary should serve them. And much more manquellers whom God bade to take from the alter and kill them, if their murder were wilful. And where it is otherwise there need we not the sanctuaries that God appointed in the old law. For if either necessity, his own defence, or misfortune draw him to that deed, a pardon serveth which either the law granteth of course, or the King of pity may.

Then look me now how few sanctuary men there be, whom any favourable necessity compelled to go thither. And then see on the other side what a sort there be commonly therein, of them whom wilful unthriftiness hath brought to nought.

What a rabble of thieves, murderers, and malicious heinous traitors, and that in two places specially. The one at the elbow of the City, the other in the very bowels. I dare well avow it, weigh the good that they do, with the hurt that cometh of them, and ye shall find it much better to lack both, than have both. And this I say, although they were not abused as they now be, and so long have be, that I fear me ever they will be while men be afeared to set their hands to the mendement: as though God and Saint Peter were the Patrons of ungracious living.

Now unthrifts riot and run in debt upon the boldness of these places: yea and rich men run thither with poor men's goods, there they build, there they spend and bid their creditors go whistle them. Men's wives run thither with their husband's plate, and say, they dare not abide with their husbands for beating. Thieves bring thither their stolen goods, and there live thereon. There devise they new robberies, nightly they steal out, they rob and reave, and kill, and come in again as though those places gave them not only a safeguard for the harm they have done, but a licence also to do more. Howbeit much of this mischief if wise men would set their hands to, it might be amended, with great thank of God and no breach of the privilege. The residue sith so long ago I wot near what Pope and what Prince more piteous than politic: hath granted it and other men since of a certain religious fear have not broken it, let us take a pain therewith, and let it a God's name stand in force, as farforth as reason will. Which is not fully so farforth, as may serve to let us of the fetching forth of this noble man to his honour and wealth, out of that place in which he neither is, nor can be a Sanctuary man.

A Sanctuary serveth always to defend the body of that man that standeth in danger abroad, not of great hurt only, but also of lawful hurt. For against unlawful harms, never Pope nor King intended to privilege any one place. For that privilege hath every place. Knoweth any man any place wherein it is lawful one man to do another wrong? That no man unlawfully take hurt, that liberty, the King, the law, and very nature forbiddeth in every place, and maketh to that regard for every man every place a Sanctuary. But where a man is by lawful means in peril, there needeth he the tuition of some special privilege, which is the only ground and cause of all sanctuaries. From which necessity this noble prince is far. Whose love to his King, nature and kindred proveth, whose innocence to all the world, his tender youth proveth. And so sanctuary as for him, neither none he needeth, nor also none can have. Men come not to sanctuary as they come to baptism, to require it by their Godfathers. He must ask it himself that must have it. And reason, sith no man hath cause to have it, but whose conscience of his own fault maketh him fain need to require it, what will then hath yonder babe? which and if he had discretion to require it, if need were, I dare say would now be right angry with them that keep him there. And I would think without any scruple of conscience, without any breach of privilege, to be somewhat more homely with them that be there sanctuary men indeed. For if one go to sanctuary with another man's goods, why should not the King leaving his body at liberty, satisfy the part of his goods even within the sanctuary? For neither King nor Pope can give any place such a privilege, that it shall discharge a man of his debts being able to pay.

And with that divers of the clergy that were present, whither they said it for his pleasure, or as they thought, agreed plainly, that by the law of God and of the church the goods of a sanctuary man should be delivered in payment of his debts, and stolen goods to the owner, and only liberty reserved him to get his living with the labour of his hands. Verily (quod the Duke) I think you say very truth. And what if a man's wife will take sanctuary, because she list to run from her husband: I would ween if she can allege none other cause, he may lawfully without any displeasure to Saint Peter, take her out of S. Peter's church by the arm. And if no body may be taken out of sanctuary that sayeth he will bide there: Then if a child will take sanctuary, because he feareth to go to school, his master must let him alone. And as simple as that sample is, yet is there less reason in our case, than in that. For therein though it be a childish fear, yet is there at the leastwise some fear. And herein is there none at all. And verily I have often heard of sanctuary men. But I never heard erst of sanctuary children. And therefore as for the conclusion of my mind, who so may have deserved to need it, if they think it for their surety, let them keep it. But he cannot be no sanctuary man, that neither hath wisdom to desire it, nor malice to deserve it, whose life or liberty can by no lawful process stand in jeopardy. And he that taketh one out of sanctuary to do him good, I say plainly that he breaketh no sanctuary. When the Duke had done, the temporal men whole, and good part of the spiritual also, thinking none hurt earthly meant toward the young babe, condescended in effect, that if he were not delivered, he should be fetched. Howbeit they thought it all best, in the avoiding of all manner of rumour, that the Lord Cardinal should first assay to get him with her good will. And thereupon all the council came unto the star-chamber at Westminster. And the Lord Cardinal leaving the Protector with the council in the star-chamber, departed into the sanctuary to the Queen, with divers other Lords with him, were it for the respect of his honour, or that she should by presence of so many perceive that this errand was not one man's mind, or were it for that the Protector intended not in this matter to trust any one man alone, or else that if she finally were determined to keep him, some of that company had haply secret instruction incontinent maugre her mind to take him and to leave her no respite to convey him, which she was likely to mind after this matter broken to her, if her time would in any wise serve her.

When the Queen and these Lords were come together in presence, the Lord Cardinal showed unto her, that it was thought unto the Protector and unto the whole council, that her keeping of the King's brother in that place was the thing which highly souned, not only to the great rumour of the people and their obloquy, but also to the importable grief and displeasure of the King's royal majesty. To whose grace it were as singular comfort, to have his natural brother in company, as it was their both dishonour and all theirs and hers also, to suffer him in sanctuary. As though the one brother stood in danger and peril of the other. And he showed her that the council therefore had sent him unto her, to require her the delivery of him, that he might be brought unto the King's presence at his liberty, out of that place which they reckoned as a prison. And there should he be demeaned according to his estate. And she in this doing should both do great good to the realm, pleasure to the council and profit to herself, succour to her friends that were in distress, and over that (which he wist well she specially tendered), not only great comfort and honour to the King, but also to the young Duke himself, whose both great wealth it were to be together, as well for many greater causes, as also for their both disport and recreation: which thing the Lord esteemed not slight, though it seem light, well pondering that their youth without recreation and play, cannot endure nor any estranger for the convenience of their both ages and estates, so meetly in that point for any of them as either of them for other.

My Lord (quod the Queen:) I say not nay, but that it were very convenient, that this gentleman whom ye require, were in the company of the King his brother. And in good faith me thinketh it were as great commodity to them both as for yet a while, to been in the custody of their mother, the tender age considered of the elder of them both, but special the younger, which besides his infancy that also needeth good looking to, hath a while been so sore diseased vexed with sickness, and is so newly rather a little amended than well recovered, that I dare put no person earthly in trust with his keeping but myself only, considering, that there is as physicians say, and as we also find, double the peril in the reciduation, that was in the first sickness, with which disease nature being forelabored, forewearied and weakened, waxeth the less able to bear out a new surfeit. And albeit there might be found other, that would haply do their best unto him: yet is there none that either knoweth better how to order him, than I that so long have kept him: or is more tenderly like to cherish him, than his own mother that bore him. No man denieth good madam (quod the Cardinal) but that your grace were of all folk most necessary about your children: and so would all the council, not only be content, but also glad that ye were, if it might stand with your pleasure to be in such place as might stand with their honour. But if you appoint yourself to tarry here, then think they yet more convenient, that the Duke of York were with the King honourably at his liberty to the comfort of them both, than here as a sanctuary man to their both dishonour and obloquy: sith there is not always so great necessity to have the child be with the mother, but that occasion may sometime be such, that it should be more expedient to keep him elsewhere. Which in this well appeareth that at such time as your dearest son then prince and now King, should for his honour and good order of the country, keep household in Wales far out of your company: your grace was well content there with yourself. Not very well content, quod the Queen: And yet the case is not like: for the one was then in health, and the other is now sick. In which case I marvel greatly that my Lord Protector is so desirous to have him in his keeping where if the child in his sickness miscarried by nature, yet might he run into slander and suspicion of fraud. And where they call it a thing so sore against my child's honour and theirs also, that he bideth in this place: it is all their honours there to suffer him bide, where no man doubteth, he shall be best kept. And that is here, while I am here, Which as yet intend not to come forth and jeopard myself after other of my friends: which would God were rather here in surety with me, than I were there in jeopardy with them. Why Madame (quod another Lord) know you any thing why they should be in jeopardy? Nay verily Sir quod she, nor why they should be in prison neither, as they now be. But it is I trow no great marvel though I fear, lest those that have not letted to put them in duress without colour, will let as little to procure their destruction without cause.

The Cardinal made a continuance to the other Lord, that he should harp no more upon that string. And then said he to the Queen, that he nothing doubted, but that those Lords of her honourable kin, which as yet remained under arrest should upon the matter examined, do well enough. And as toward her noble person, neither was nor could be, any manner jeopardy. Whereby should I trust that (quod the Queen) In that I am guiltless? As though they were guilty. In that I am with their enemies better beloved than they? When they hate them for my sake. In that I am so near of kin to the King? And how far be they off, if that would help as God send grace it hurt not. And therefore as for me, I purpose not as yet to depart hence. And as for this gentleman my son, I mind that he shall be where I am till I see further. For I assure you, for that I see some men so greedy without any substantial cause to have him, this maketh me much the more farther to deliver him. Truly Madame, quod he, and the farther that you be to deliver him, the farther been other men to suffer you to keep him, lest your causeless fear might cause you farther to convey him. And many be there that think that he can have no privilege in this place, which neither can have will to ask it, nor malice to deserve it. And therefore they reckon no privilege broken, though they fetch him out. Which if ye finally refuse to deliver him, I verily think they will. So much dread hath my Lord his uncle, for the tender love he beareth him, lest your grace should hap to send him away. A Sir quod the Queen, hath the Protector so tender zeal to him, that he feareth nothing but lest he should escape him. Thinketh he that I would send him hence, which neither is in the plight to send out, and in what place could I reckon him sure, if he be not sure in this the sanctuary whereof, was there never tyrant yet so devilish, that durst presume to break. And I trust God as strong now to withstand his adversaries, as ever he was. But my son can deserve no sanctuary, and therefore he cannot have it. Forsooth he hath found a goodly glose, by which that place that may defend a thief, may not save an innocent. But he is in no jeopardy nor hath no need thereof. Would God he had not. Troweth the Protector (I pray God he may prove a Protector) troweth he that I perceive not whereunto his painted process draweth? It is not honourable that the Duke bide here: it were comfortable for them both that he were with his brother, because the King lacketh a play-fellow be ye sure. I pray God send them both better play-fellows than him, that maketh so high a matter upon such a trifling pretext: as though there could none be found to play with the King, but if his brother that hath no lust to play for sickness, come out of sanctuary out of his safeguard, to play with him. As though princes as young as they be, could not play but with their peers, or children could not play but with their kindred, with whom for the more part they agree much worse than with strangers. But the child cannot require the privilege, who told him so? he shall here him ask it and he will.

Howbeit this is a gay matter: Suppose he could not ask it, suppose he would not ask it, suppose he would ask to go out, if I say he shall not, if I ask the privilege but for myself, I say he that against my will taketh out him, breaketh the sanctuary. Serveth this liberty for my person only, or for my goods too? ye may not hence take my horse from me: and may you take my child from me? he is also my ward, for as my learned council showeth me, sith he hath nothing by descent holden by knight's service, the law maketh, his mother his guardian. Then may no man, I suppose take my ward from me out of sanctuary, without the breach of the sanctuary. And if my privilege could not serve him, nor he ask it for himself, yet sith the law committeth to me the custody of him, I may require it for him, except the law give a child a guardian only for his goods and his lands, discharging him of the cure and safe keeping of his body, for which only both lands and goods serve.

And if examples be sufficient to obtain privilege for my child, I need not far to seeke. For in this place in which we now be (and which is now in question whither my child may take benefit of it) mine other son now King was born, and kept in his cradle, and preserved to a more prosperous fortune, which I pray God long to continue. And as all you know, this is not the first time that I have taken sanctuary, for when my Lord my husband was banished and thrust out of his kingdom, I fled hither being great with child, and here I bore the Prince. And when my Lord my husband returned safe again and had the victory, then went I hence to welcome him home, and from hence I brought my babe the Prince unto his father, when he first took him in his arms. And I pray God that my son's palace may be as great safeguard to him now reigning, as this place was sometime to the King's enemy. In which place I intend to keep his brother sith, &c.

Wherefore here intend I to keep him since man's law serveth the guardian to keep the infant. The law of nature will the mother keep her child. God's law privilegeth the sanctuary, and the sanctuary my son, sith I fear to put him in the protector's hands that hath his brother already, and were if both failed, inheritor to the crown. The cause of my fear hath no man to do to examine. And yet fear I no further than the law feareth which as learned men tell me forbiddeth every man the custody of them, by whose death he may inherit less land than a Kingdome. I can no more, but whosoever he be that breaketh this holy sanctuary: I pray God shortly send him need of sanctuary, when he may not come to it. For taken out of sanctuary would I not my mortal enemy were.

The Lord Cardinal perceiving that the Queen waxed ever the longer the farther off, and also that she began to kindle and chafe, and speak sore biting words against the Protector, and such as he neither believed, and was also loath to hear, he said unto her for a final conclusion, that he would no longer dispute the matter. But if she were content to deliver the Duke to him and to the other Lords there present, he durst lay his own body and soul both in pledge, not only for his surety but also for his estate. And if she would give them a resolute answer to the contrary, he would forthwith depart there with all, and shift whoso would with this business afterwards: for he never intended more to move her in that matter, in which she thought that he and all other save herself, lacked either wit or truth. Wit if they were so dull, that they could nothing perceive what the Protector intended: truth if they should procure her son to be delivered into his hands , in whom they should perceive toward the child any evil intended.

The Queen with these words stood a good while in a great study. And forasmuch her seemed the Cardinal more ready to depart, than some of the remnant, and the Protector himself ready at hand, so that she verily thought she could not keep him there, but that he should incontinent be taken thence: and to convey him elsewhere, neither had she time to serve her, nor place determined, nor persons appointed, all thing unready this message came on her so suddenly, nothing less looking for them to have him fetched out of sanctuary, which she thought to be now beset in such places about, that he could not be conveyed out untaken, and partly as she thought it might fortune her fear to be false, so will she waste it was either needless or bootless: wherefore if she should needs go from him, she deemed it best to deliver him. And over that of the Cardinal's faith she nothing doubted, nor of some other Lords neither, whom she there saw. Which as she feared lest they might be deceived: so was she well assured they would not be corrupted: Then thought she it should yet make them the more warily to look to him, and the more circumspectly to see to his surety, if she with her own hands betook him to them of trust. And at the last she took the young Duke by the hand, and said unto the Lords: my Lord (quod she) and all my Lords, I neither am so unwise to mistrust your wits, nor so suspicious to mistrust your truths. Of which I purpose to make you such a proof, as if either of both lacked in you, might turn both me to great sorrow, the realm to much harm, and you to great reproach. For lo here is (quod she) this gentleman, whom I doubt not but I could here keep safe if I would, whatsoever any man say. And I doubt not also but there be some abroad so deadly enemies unto my blood, that if they wist where any of it lay in their own body, they would let it out. We have also had experience that the desire of a kingdom knoweth no kindred. The brother hath been the brother's bane. And may the nephews be sure of their uncle? Each of these children is other's defence while they be asunder, and each of their lives lieth in the other's body. Keep one safe and both be sure, and nothing for them both more perilous, than to be both in one place. For what wise merchant adventureth all his good in one ship? All this notwithstanding, here I deliver him and his brother in him, to keep into your hands , of whom I shall ask them both afore God and the world. Faithful ye be that wot I well and I know well you be wise. Power and strength to keep him if ye list neither lack ye of yourself, nor can lack help in this cause. And if ye cannot else where, then may you leave him here. But only one thing I beseech you for the trust that his father put in you ever, and for trust that I put in you now, that as far as ye think that I fear to much, be you well ware that to fear not as far to little. And therewithal she said unto the child: farewell my own sweet son, God send you good keeping, let me kiss you once yet ere you go, for God knoweth when we shall kiss together again. And therewith she kissed him, and blessed him, turned her back and wept and went her way, leaving the child weeping as fast. When the Lord Cardinal and these other Lords with him, had received this young Duke, they brought him into the star-chamber where the Protector took him in his arms and kissed him with these words:

Now welcome my Lord even with all my very heart. And he said in that of likelihood as he thought. Thereupon forthwith they brought him to the King his brother into the bishops palace at Paul's, and from thence through the city honourably into the tower, out of which after that day they never came abroad.

When the Protector had both the children in his hands , he opened himself more boldly, both to certain other men, and also chiefly to the Duke of Buckingham. Although I know that many thought, that this Duke was privy to all the Protector's council, even from the beginning. And some of the Protector's friends said, that the Duke was the first mover of the Protector to this matter, sending a privy messenger unto him, straight after King Edward's death. But other again which knew better the subtle wit of the Protector, deny that he ever opened his enterprise to the Duke, until he had brought to pass the things before rehearsed. But when he had imprisoned the Queen's kinsfolk, and gotten both her sons into his own hands, than he opened the rest of his purpose with less fear to them whom he thought meet for the matter, and specially to the Duke: who being won to his purpose, he thought his strength more than half increased. The matter was broken unto the Duke, by subtle folks , and such as were their craft masters in the handling of such wicked devices: who declared unto him, that the young King was offended with him for his kinsfolk's sakes, and that if he were ever able, he would revenge them. Who would prick him forward thereunto, if they escaped (for they would remember their imprisonment). Or else if they were put to death, without doubt the young King would be careful for their deaths, whose imprisonment was grievous unto him. And that with repenting the Duke should nothing avail: for there was no way left to redeem his offence by benefits: but he should sooner destroy himself than save the King, who with his brother and his kinsfolk he saw in such places imprisoned, as the Protector might with a beck destroy them all: and that it were no doubt but he would do it indeed, if there were any new enterprise attempted. And that it was likely that as the Protector had provided privy guard for himself, so had he spials for the Duke, and trains to catch him, if he should be against him, and that peradventure from them, whom he least suspected. For the state of things and the dispositions of men were then such, that a man could not well tell whom he might trust, or whom he might fear. These things and such like, being beaten into the Duke's mind, brought him to that point, that where he had repented the way that he had entered, yet would he go forth in the same: and since he had once begun, he would stoutly go through. And therefore to this wicked enterprise, which he believed could not be voided, he bent himself and went through: and determined, that since the common mischief could not be amended, he would turn it as much as he might to his own commodity.

Then it was agreed, that the Protector should have the Duke's aid to make him King, and that the Protector's only lawful son, should marry the Duke's daughter, and that the Protector should grant him the quiet possession of the Earldom of Hertford, which he claimed as his inheritance, and could never obtain it in King Edward's time. Besides these requests of the Duke, the Protector of his own mind promised him a great quantity of the King's treasure and of his household stuff. And when they were thus at a point between themselves, they went about to prepare for the coronation of the young King as they would have it seem. And that they might turn both the eyes and minds of men, from perceiving of their drifts other where the Lords being sent for from all parts of the realm, came thick to that solemnity. But the

Protector and the Duke, after that, that they had set the Lord Cardinal, the Archbishop of York then Lord Chancellor, the Bishop of Ely, the Lord Stanley and the Lord Hastings then Lord Chamberlain, with many other noble men to commune and devise about the coronation in one place: as fast were they in another place contriving the contrary, and to make the Protector King. To which council, albeit there were adhibit very few, and they very secret: yet began there here and there about, some manner of muttering among the people, as though all should not long be well, though they neither wist what they feared nor wherefore: were it that before such great things, men's hearts of a secret instinct of nature misgiveth them. As the sea without wind swelleth of himself sometime before a tempest: or were it that some one man haply somewhat perceiving, filled many men with suspicion, though he showed few men what he knew. Howbeit somewhat the dealing self made men to muse on the matter, though the council were close. For little and little all folk withdrew from the Tower, and drew to Crosbie's place in Bishopsgate Street where the Protector kept his household. The Protector had the resort, the King in manner desolate. While some for their business made suit to them that had the doing, some were by their friends secretly warned, that it might haply turn them to no good, to be to much attendant about the King without the Protector's appointment: which removed also divers of the prince's old servants from him, and set new about him. Thus many things coming together partly by chance, partly of purpose, caused at length, not common people that wave with the wind, but wise men also and so Lords, yeke to mark the matter and muse thereon: so farforth that the Lord Stanley, that was after Earl of Darby, wisely mistrusted it, and said unto the Lord Hastings, that he much misliked these two several councils. For while we (quod he) talk of one matter in the one place, little wot we whereof they talk in the other place. My Lord (quod the Lord Hastings) on my life never doubt you. For while one man is there which is never thence, never can there be thing once minded that should sound amiss toward me, but it should be in mine ears ere it were well out of their mouths. This meant he by Catesby, which was of his near secret counsel, and whom he very familiarly used, and in his most weighty matters put no man in so special trust, reckoning himself to no man so lief, sith he well wist there was no man to him so much beholden as was this Catesby, which was a man well learned in the laws of this land, and by the special favour of the Lord Chamberlain, in good authority and much rule bore in all the county of Leicester where the Lord

Chamberlain's power chiefly lay. But surely great pity was it, that he had not had either more truth or less wit. For his dissimulation only, kept all that mischief up. In whom if the Lord Hastings had not put so special trust, the Lord Stanley and he had departed with divers other Lords, and broken all the dance, for many ill signs that he saw, which he now construes all to the best. So surely thought he that there could be none harm toward him in that council intended where Catesby was. And of truth the Protector and the Duke of Buckingham made very good semblance unto the Lord Hastings, and kept him much in company. And undoubtedly the Protector loved him well, and loath was to have lost him, saving for fear lest his life should have quailed their purpose. For which cause he moved Catesby to prove with some words cast out afar off, whither he could think it possible to win the Lord Hasting into their part. But Catesby whither he assayed him or assayed him not, reported unto them, that he found him so fast, and hard him speak so terrible words, that he durst no further break. And of truth the Lord Chamberlain of very trust showed unto Catesby, the mistrust that other began to have in the matter. And therefore he fearing lest their motions might with the Lord Hastings minish his credence, whereunto only all the matter leaned, procured the Protector hastily to rid him. And much the rather, for that he trusted by his death to obtain much of the rule that the Lord Hastings bore in his country: the only desire whereof, was the allective that induced him to be partner and one special contriver of all this horrible treason.

Whereupon soon after that is to wit, on the Friday the thirteenth day of June many Lords assembled in the tower, and there sat in council, devising the honourable solemnity of the King's coronation, of which the time appointed so near approached, that the pageants and subtleties were in making day and night at Westminster, and much victual killed therefore, that afterward was cast away. These Lords so sitting together communing of this matter, the Protector came in among them, first about nine of the clock, saluting them courteously, and excusing himself that he had been from them so long, saying merely that he had been asleep that day. And after a little talking with them, he said unto the Bishop of Ely: my Lord you have very good strawberries at your garden in Holborn, I require you let us have a mess of them. Gladly my Lord, quod he, would God I had some better thing as ready to your pleasure as that. And therewith in all the haste he sent his servant for a mess of strawberries. The Protector set the Lords fast in communing, and thereupon praying them to spare him for a little while, departed thence. And soon after one hour between ten and eleven he returned into the chamber among them, all changed with a wonderful sore angry countenance, knitting the brows, frowning and fretting and knawing on his lips and so sat him down, in his place: all the Lords much dismayed and sore marvelling of this manner of sudden change, and what thing should him ail. Then when he had sitten still a while, thus he began: what were they worthy to have, that compass and imagine the destruction of me, being so near of blood unto the King and Protector of his royal person and his realm. At this question, all the Lords sat sore astonied, musing much by whom this question should be meant, of which every man wist himself clear. Then the Lord Chamberlain, as he that for the love between them thought he might be boldest with him, answered and said, that they were worthy to be punished as heinous traitors whatsoever they were. And all the other affirmed the same. That is (quod he) yonder sorceress my brother's wife and other with her meaning the Queen. At these words many of the other Lords were greatly abashed that favoured her. But the Lord Hastings was in his mind better content, that it was moved by her, than by any other whom he loved better: Albeit his heart somewhat grudged, that he was not afore, made of council in this matter as he was of the taking of her kindred, and of their putting to death, which were by his assent before, devised to be beheaded at Pontefract, this self same day, in which he was not ware that it was by other devised, that himself should the same day be beheaded at London. Then said the Protector: ye shall all se in what wise that sorceress and that other witch of her council Shore's wife with their affinity, have by their sorcery and witchcraft wasted my body. And therewith he plucked up his doublet sleeve to his elbow upon his left arm, where he showed a wearish withered arm and small, as it was never other. And thereupon every man's mind sore misgave them, well perceiving that this matter was but a quarrel. For well they wist, that the Queen was too wise to go about any such folly. And also if she would, yet would she of all folk least make Shore's wife of counsel, whom of all women she most hated, as that concubine whom the King her husband had most loved. And also no man was there present, but well knew that his arm was ever such since his birth. Natheless the Lord Chamberlain (which from the death of King Edward kept Shore's wife, on whom he somewhat doted in the

King's life, saving as it is said he that while forbore her of reverence toward his King, or else of a certain kind of fidelity to his friend) answered and said: certainly my Lord if they have so heinously done, and they be worthy heinous punishment. What quod the Protector thou servest me I ween with ifs and with ands, I tell the they have so done, and that I will make good on thy body traitor. And therewith as in a great anger, he clapped his fist upon the board a great rap. At which token given, one cried treason without the chamber. Therewith a door clapped, and in come there rushing men in harness as many as the chamber might hold. And anon the Protector said to the Lord Hastings: I arrest thee traitor. What me my Lord quod he. Yea the traitor, quod the
Protector.

And another let fly at the Lord Stanley which shrunk at the stroke and fell under the table, or else his head had been cleft to the teeth: for as shortly as he shrank, yet ran the blood about his ears. Then were they all quickly bestowed in divers chambers, except the Lord Chamberlain, whom the Protector bade speed and shrive him apace, for by saint Paul (quod he) I will not to dinner till I see thy head off. It booted him not to ask why but heavily he took a priest at adventure, and made a short shrift, for a longer would not be suffered, the Protector made so much haste to dinner: which he might not go to till this were done for the saving of his oath.

So was he brought forth into the green beside the chapel within the tower, and his head laid down upon a long log of timber, and there stricken off, and afterward his body with the head entered at Windsor beside the body of King Edward, whose both souls our Lord pardon.

A marvellous case is it to hear, either the warnings of that he should have voided, or the tokens of that he could not void. For the self night next before his death, the Lord Stanley sent a trusty secret messenger unto him at midnight in all the haste, requiring him to rise and ride away with him, for he was disposed utterly no longer to bide: he had so fearful a dream, in which him thought that a boar with his tusks so raced them both by the heads, that the blood ran about both their shoulders. And forasmuch as the Protector gave the boar for his cognisance, this dream made so fearful an impression in his heart, that he was thoroughly determined no longer to tarry, but had his horse ready, if the Lord Hastings would go with him to ride so far yet the same night, that they should be out of danger ere day. Ay good Lord quod the Lord Hastings to this messenger, leaneth my Lord thy master so much to such trifles, and hath such faith in dreams, which either his own fear fantasieth or do rise in the night's rest by reason of his day thoughts? Tell him it is plain witchcraft to believe in such dreams: which if they were tokens of things to come, why thinketh he not that we might be as likely to make them true by our going if we were caught and brought back (as friends fail fleers) for then had the boar a cause likely to race us with his tusks, as folk that fled for some falsehood, wherefore either is there no peril, nor none there is in deed: or if any be, it is rather in going than biding. And if we should needs cost fall in peril one way or other: yet had I lever that men should see it were by other men's falsehood, than think it were either our own fault or faint heart. And therefore go to thy master man, and commend me to him and pray him be merry and have no fear: for I ensure him I am as sure of the man that he wotteth of, as I am of my own hand. God send grace Sir quod the messenger, and went his way.

Certain is it also, that in the riding toward the tower, the same morning in which he was beheaded, his horse twice or thrice stumbled with him almost to the falling, which thing albeit each man wot well daily happeneth to them to whom no such mischance is toward: yet hath it been of an old rite and custom, observed as a token often times notably foregoing some great misfortune. Now this that followeth was no warning, but an enemious scorned. The same morning ere he were up, came a knight unto him, as it were of courtesy to accompany him to the council, but of truth sent by the Protector to haste him thitherward, with whom he was of secret confederacy in that purpose, a mean man at that time, and now of great authority . This knight when it happed the Lord Chamberlain by the way to stay his horse, and commune a while with a priest whom he met in the Tower Street, broke his tale and said merely to him: what my Lord I pray you come on, whereto talk you so long with that priest, you have no need of a priest yet: and therewith he laughed upon him, as though he would say, ye shall have soon. But so little wist the other what he meant, and so little mistrusted, that he was never merrier nor never so full of good hope in his life: which self thing is often seen a sign of change. But I shall rather let any thing pass me, than the vain surety of man's mind so near his death. Upon the very tower wharf so near the place where his head was off so soon after, there met he with one Hastings a pursuivant of his own name. And of their meeting in that place, he was put in remembrance of another time, in which it had happened them before, to meet in like manner together in the same place. At which other time the Lord Chamberlain had been accused unto King Edward, by the Lord Rivers the Queen's brother, in such wise that he was for the while (but it lasted not long) far fallen into the King's indignation, and stood in great fear of himself. And forasmuch as he now met this pursuivant in the same place that jeopardy so well passed: it gave him great pleasure to talk with him thereof with whom he had before talked thereof, in the same place while he was therein. And therefore he said: Ah Hastings, art you remembered when I met thee here once with an heavy heart: Yea my Lord (quod he) that remember I well, and thanked be God they got no good, nor ye none harm thereby. Thou wouldest say so quod he, if thou knewest as much as I know, which few know else as yet and more shall shortly. That meant he by the Lords of the Queen's kindred that were taken before, and should that day be beheaded at Pontefract: which he well wist, but nothing ware that the axe hang over his own head. In faith man quod he, I was never so sorry, nor never stood in so great dread in my life, as I did when thou and I met here. And lo how the world is turned, now stand mine enemies in that danger (as thou mayest hap to hear more hereafter) and I never in my life so merry, nor never in so great surety. O good God, the blindness of our mortal nature, when he most feared, he was in good surety: when he reckoned himself surest, he lost his life, and that within two hours after. Thus ended this honourable man, a good knight and a gentle, of great authority with his prince, of living somewhat desolate, plain and open to his enemy, and secret to his friend: ethe to beguile, as he that of good heart and courage forestudied no perils. A loving man and passing well beloved. Very faithful, and trusty enough, trusting to much.

Now flew the fame of this Lord's death, swiftly through the city, and so forth farther about like a wind in every man's ear. But the Protector immediately after dinner, intending to set some colour upon the matter, sent in all the haste for many substantial men out of the city into the Tower. And at their coming, himself with the Duke of Buckingham, stood harnessed in old ill faring briganders, such as no man should ween that they would vouchsafe to have put upon their backs, except that some sudden necessity had constrained them. And then the Protector showed them, that the Lord Chamberlain, and other of his conspiracy, had contrived to have suddenly destroyed him and the Duke, there the same day in the council. And what they intended further, was as yet not well known. Of which their treason he never had knowledge before ten of the clock the same forenoon. Which sudden fear drove them to put on for their defence such harness as came next to hand. And so had God holpen them, that the mischief turned upon them that would have done it. And this he required them to report. Every man answered him fair, as though no man mistrusted the matter which of truth no man believed. Yet for the further appeasing of the people's mind, he sent immediately after diner in all the haste, one herald of arms, with a proclamation to be made through the city in the King's name, containing that the Lord Hastings with divers other of his traitorous purpose, had before conspired the same day, to have slain the Lord Protector and the Duke of Buckingham sitting in the council, and after to have taken upon them to rule the King and the realm at their pleasure, and thereby to pill and spoil whom they list uncontrolled. And much matter was there in the proclamation devised, to the slander of the Lord Chamberlain, as that he was an evil counsellor to the King's father, enticing him to many things highly redounding to the minishing of his honour, and to the universal hurt of his realm, by his evil company, sinister procuring, and ungracious ensample, as well in many other things as in the vicious living and inordinate abusion of his body, both with many other, and also specially with Shore's wife, which was one also of his most secret council of this heinous treason, with whom he lay nightly, and namely the night last passed next before his death, so that it was the less marvel, if ungracious living brought him to an unhappy ending: which he was now put unto, by the most dread commandment of the King's highness and of his honourable and faithful council, both for his demerits, being so openly taken in his falsely conceived treason, and also lest the delaying of his execution, might have encouraged other mischievous persons partners of his conspiracy, to gather and assemble themselves together in making some great commotion for his deliverance, whose hope now being by his well deserved death politically repressed, all the realm should by God's grace rest in good quiet and peace. Now was this proclamation made within two hours after that he was beheaded, and it was so curiously indicted, and so fair written in parchment in so well a set hand, and therewith of itself so long a process, that every child might well perceive, that it was prepared before. For all the time between his death and the proclaiming could scant have sufficed unto the bare writing alone, all had it been but in paper and scribbled forth in haste at adventure. So that upon the proclaiming thereof, one that was school master of Paul's of chance standing by, and comparing the shortness of the time with the length of the matter, said unto them that stood about him here is a gay goodly cast, foul cast away for haste. And a merchant answered him, that it was written by prophesy.

Now then by and by, as it were for anger not for covetise, the Protector sent into the house of Shore's wife (for her husband dwelled not with her) and spoiled her of all that ever she had, above the value of two or three thousand marks, and sent her body to prison. And when he had a while laid unto her for the manner sake, that she went about to bewitch him, and that she was of council with the Lord Chamberlain to destroy him: in conclusion, when that no colour could fasten upon these matters, then he laid heinously to her charge, and the thing that she herself could not deny, that all the world wist was true, and that natheless every man laughed at to hear it then so suddenly so highly taken, that she was naught of her body. And for this cause (as a goodly continent prince clean and faultless of himself, sent out of heaven into this vicious world for the amendment of men's manners) he caused the Bishop of London to put her to open penance, going before the cross in procession upon a Sunday with a taper in her hand. In which she went in countenance and pace demure so womanly, and albeit she were out of all array save her kirtle only: yet went she so fair and lovely, namely while the wondering of the people cast a comely red in her cheeks (of which she before had most missed) that her great shame won her much praise, among those that were more amorous of her body than curious of her soul. And many good folk also that hated her living, and glad were to see sin corrected: yet pitied they more her penance, than rejoiced therein, when they considered that the Protector procured it, more of a corrupt intent than any virtuous affection.

This woman was born in London, worshipfully friended, honestly brought up, and very well married, saving somewhat too soon, her husband an honest citizen, young and goodly and of good substance. But forasmuch as they were coupled ere she were well ripe, she not very fervently loved, for whom she never longed. Which was haply the thing, that the more easily made her incline unto the King's appetite when he required her. Howbeit the respect of his royalty, the hope of gay apparel, ease, pleasure and other wanton wealth, was able soon to pierce a soft tender heart. But when the King had abused her, anon her husband (as he was an honest man and one that could his good, not presuming to touch a King's concubine) left her up to him all together. When the King died, the Lord Chamberlain took her. Which in the King's days, albeit he was sore enamoured upon her, yet he forbore her, either for reverence, or for a certain friendly faithfulness. Proper she was and fair: nothing in her body that you would have changed, but if you would have wished her somewhat higher. Thus say they that knew her in her youth. Albeit some that now see her (for yet she liveth) deem her never to have been well visaged. Whose judgement seemeth me somewhat like, as though men should guess the beauty of one long before departed, by her scalp taken out of the charnel house: for now is she old lean, withered and dried up, nothing left but rivelled skin and hard bone. And yet being even such: whoso well advise her visage, might guess and devise which parts now filled, would make it a fair face. Yet she delighted not men so much in her beauty, as in her pleasant behaviour. For a proper wit had she, and could both read well and write, merry in company, ready and quick of answer, neither mute nor full of babble, sometime taunting without displeasure not without disport.

The King would say that he had three concubines, which in three divers properties diversely excelled. One the merriest, another the wiliest, the third the holiest harlot in his realm, as one whom no man could get out of the church lightly to any place, but it were to his bed. The other two were somewhat greater parsonages, and natheless of their humility content to be nameless, and to forbear the praise of those properties. But the merriest was this Shore's wife, in whom the King therefore took special pleasure. For many he had, but her he loved, whose favour to say the truth (for sin it were to belie the devil) she never abused to any man's hurt, but to many a man's comfort and relief: where the King took displeasure, she would mitigate and appease his mind: where men were out of favour, she would bring them in his grace. For many that had highly offended, she obtained pardon. Of great forfeitures she got men remission. And finally in many weighty suits, she stood many men in great stead, either for none, or very small rewards, and those rather gay than rich: either for that she was content with the deed self well done, or for that she delighted to be sued unto, and to show what she was able to do with the King, or for that wanton women and wealthy be not always covetous. I doubt not some shall think this woman too slight a thing, to be written of and set among the remembrances of great matters: which they shall specially think, that haply shall esteem her only by that they now see her. But me seemeth the chance so much the more worthy to be remembered, in how much she is now in the more beggarly condition, unfriended and worn out of acquaintance, after good substance, after as great favour with the prince, after as great suit and seeking to with all those that those days had business to speed, as many other men were in their times, which be now famous, only by the infamy of their ill deeds. Her doings were not much less, albeit they be much less remembered, because they were not so evil. For men use if they have an evil turn, to write it in marble: and whoso doth us a good turn, we write it in dust which is not worst proved by her: for at this day she beggeth of many at this day living, that at this day had begged if she had not been.

Now was it so devised by the Protector and his council, that the self day in which the Lord Chamberlain was beheaded in the tower of London, and about the selfsame hour, was there not without his assent beheaded at Pontefract, the fore remembered Lords and knights that were taken from the King at Northampton and Stony Stratford. Which thing was done in the presence and by the order of Sir Richard Ratcliff knight, whose service the Protector specially used in the council and in the execution of such lawless enterprises, as a man that had been long secret with him, having experience of the world and a shrewd wit, short and rude in speech, rough and boistious of behaviour, bold in mischief, as far from pity as from all fear of God. This knight bringing them out of the prison to the scaffold, and showing to the people about that they were traitors, not suffering them to speak and declare their innocence lest their words might have inclined men to pity them, and to hate the Protector and his part: caused them hastily without judgement, process, or manner of order to be beheaded, and without other earthly guilt, but only that they were good men, to be true to the King and to nigh to the Queen.

Now when the Lord Chamberlain and these other Lords were thus beheaded and rid out of the way: then thought the Protector, that while men mused what the matter meant, while the Lords of the realm were about him out of their own strengths, while no man wist what to think nor whom to trust, ere ever they should have space to dispute and digest the matter and make parties: it were best hastily to pursue his purpose, and put himself in possession of the crown, ere men could have time to devise any ways to resist. But now was all the study, by what mean this matter being of itself so heinous, might be first broken to the people, in such wise that it might be well taken. To this council they took divers, such as they thought meetly to be trusted, likely to be induced to the part, and able to stand them in stead, either by power or policy.

Among whom, they made of Council Edmund Shaw knight then Mayor of London, which upon trust of his own advancement, whereof he was of a proud heart highly desirous, should frame the city to their appetite. Of spiritual men they took such as had wit, and were in authority among the people for opinion of their learning, and had no scrupulous conscience.

Among these had they John Shaw clerk brother to the Mayor, and friar Penker provincial of the Augustine friars both doctors of divinity, both great preachers, both of more learning than virtue, of more fame than learning. For they were before greatly esteemed among the people: but after that never. Of these two the one had a sermon in praise of the Protector before the coronation, the other after, both so full of tedious flattery, that no man's ears could abide them. Penker in his sermon so lost his voice that he was fain to leave off and come down in the midst. Doctor Shaw by his sermon lost his honesty, and soon after his life, for very shame of the world, into which he durst never after come abroad. But the friar forced for no shame, and so it harmed him the less. Howbeit some doubt and many think, that Penker was not of council of the matter before the coronation, but after the common manner fell to flattery after: namely sith his sermon was not incontinent upon it, but at S. Mary Hospital at the Easter after. But certain is it, that Doctor Shaw was of council in the beginning, so far forth that they determined that he should first break the matter in a sermon at Paul's Cross, in which he should by the authority of his preaching, incline the people to the Protector's ghostly purpose. But now was all the labour and study, in the devise of some convenient pretext, for which the people should be content, to depose the prince and accept the Protector for King. In which divers things they devised. But the chief thing and the weighty of all that invention, rested in this that they should allege bastardy, either in King Edward himself, or in his children, or both. So that he should seem disabled to inherit the crown by the Duke of York, and the prince by him. To lay bastardy in King Edward, sounded openly to the rebuke of the Protector's own mother, which was mother to them both: for in that point could be none other colour, but to pretend that his own mother was one adulteress which not withstanding to further this purpose he letted not: but natheless he would the point should be less and more favourably handled, not even fully plain and directly, but that the matter should be touched aslope craftily, as though men spared in that point to speak all the truth for fear of his displeasure. But the other point concerning the bastardy that they devised to surmise in King Edward's children, that would he should be openly declared and enforced to the uttermost. The colour and pretext whereof cannot be well perceived, but if we first repeat you some things long before done about King Edward's marriage.

After that King Edward the fourth had deposed King Henry the sixth, and was in peaceable possession of the realm, determining himself to marry, as it was requisite both for himself and for the realm, he sent over in embassiate, the Earl of Warwick with other noble men in his company unto Spain, to entreat and conclude a marriage between King Edward and the King's daughter of Spain. In which thing the Earl of Warwick found the parties so toward and willing, that he speedily according to his instructions, without any difficulty brought the matter to very good conclusion.

Now happed it that in the mean season, there came to make a suit by petition to the King, Dame Elizabeth Gray which was after his Queen, at that time a widow borne of noble blood, specially by her mother, which was Duchess of Bedford ere she married the Lord

Woodfield her father. Howbeit this Dame Elizabeth herself being in service with Queen Margaret, wife unto King Henry the sixth was married unto one John Gray a squire whom King Henry made knight upon the field that he had on Shrove Tuesday at Saint Alban's against King Edward. And little while enjoyed he that knighthood, for he was at the same field slain. After which done, and the Earl of Warwick being in his embassiate about the afore remembered marriage, this poor lady made humble suit unto the King, that she might be restored unto such small lands as her late husband had given her in jointure. Whom when the King beheld, and heard her speak, as she was both fair, of a good favour, moderate of stature, well made and very wise: he not only pitied her, but also waxed enamoured on her. And taking her afterward secretly aside, began to enter in talking more familiarly. Whose appetite when she perceived, she virtuously denied him. But that did she so wisely, and with so good manner, and words so well set, that she rather kindled his desire than quenched it. And finally after many a meeting, much wooing and many great promises, she well espied the King's affection toward her so greatly increased, that she durst somewhat the more boldly say her mind, as to him whose heart she perceived more firmly set, than to fall off for a word. And in conclusion she showed him plain, that as she wist herself too simple to be his wife, so thought she herself too good to be his concubine. The King much marvelling of her constancy, as he that had not been wont elsewhere to be so stiffly said nay, so much esteemed her continence and chastity, that he set her virtue in the stead of possession and riches. And thus taking council of his desire, determined in all possible haste to marry her. And after he was thus appointed, and had between them twain ensured her: then asked he council of his other friends, and that in such manner, as they might ethe perceive it booted not greatly to say nay.

Notwithstanding the Duchess of York his mother was so sore moved therewith, that she dissuaded the marriage as much as she possibly might alleging that it was in his honour, profit, and surety also, to marry in a noble progeny out of his realm, whereupon depended great strength to his estate by the affinity and great possibility of increase of his possessions. And that he could not well otherwise do, standing that the Earl of Warwick had so far moved already. Which were not likely to take it well, if all his voyage were in such wise frustrate, and his appointments deluded. And she said also that it was not princely to marry his own subject, no great occasion leading thereunto, no possessions, or other commodities, depending thereupon, but only as it were a rich man that would marry his maid, only for a little wanton dotage upon her person. In which marriage many more commend the maiden's fortune, than the master's wisdom. And yet therein she said was more honesty, than honour in this marriage. Forasmuch as there is between no merchant and his own maid so great difference, as between the King and this widow. In whose person albeit there was nothing to be misliked, yet was there she said: nothing so excellent, but it might be found in divers other, that were more meetly (quod she) for your estate, and maidens also, whereas the only widowhood of Elizabeth Gray though she were in all other things convenient for you, should yet suffice as me seemeth to refrain you from her marriage, sith it is an unfitting thing, and a very blemish, and high disparagement, to the sacred majesty of a prince, that ought as nigh to approach priesthood in cleanness as he doth in dignity, to be defouled with bigamy in his first marriage.

The King when his mother had said, made her answer part in earnest part in play merely, as he that wist himself out of her rule. And albeit he would gladly that she should take it well, yet was at a point in his own mind, took she it well or otherwise. Howbeit somewhat to satisfy her he said, that albeit marriage being a spiritual thing, ought rather to be made for the respect of God where his grace inclineth the parties to love together as he trusted it was in his than for the regard of any temporal advantage: yet natheless him seemed that this marriage even worldly considered, was not unprofitable. For he reckoned the amity of no earthly nation so necessary for him, as the friendship of his own. Which he thought likely to bear him so much the more hearty favour in that he disdained not to marry with one of his own land. And yet if outward alliance were thought so requisite, he would find the means to enter thereinto, much better by other of his kin, where all the parties could be contented, than to marry himself, whom he should haply never love, and for the possibility of more possessions, lose the fruit and pleasure of this that he had already. For small pleasure taketh a man of all that ever he hath beside, if he be wived against his appetite. And I doubt not quod he but there be as ye say other, that be in every point comparable with her. And therefore I let not them that like them to wed them. No more is it reason that it mislike any man, that I marry where it liketh me. And I am sure that my cousin of Warwick neither loveth me so little, to grudge at that I love, nor is so unreasonable to look that I should in choice of a wife, rather then be ruled by his eye, than by mine own: as though I were a ward that were bound to marry by the appointment of a guardian. I would not be a King with that condition, to forbear mine own liberty in choice of my own marriage. As for possibility of more inheritance by new affinity in strange lands, is oft the occasion of more trouble than profit. And we have already title by that means, to so much as sufficeth to get and keep well in one man's days. That she is a widow and hath already children, by God's blessed Lady I am a bachelor and have some too: and so each of us hath a proof that neither of us is like to be barren. And therefore madam I pray you be content, I trust in God she shall bring forth a young prince, that shall please you. And as for the bigamy, let the bishop hardly lay it in my way, when I come to take orders. For I understand it is forbidden a priest, but I never wist it yet that it was forbidden a prince. The Duchess with these words nothing appeased, and seeing the King so set thereon that she could not pull him back, so highly she disdained it, that under pretext of her duty to Godward, she devised to disturb this marriage, and rather to help that he should marry one Dame Elizabeth Lucy, whom the King had also not long before gotten with child. Wherefore the King's mother objected openly against his marriage, as it were in discharge of her conscience, that the King was sure to Dame Elizabeth Lucy and her husband before God. By reason of which words, such obstacle was made in the matter, that either the Bishops durst not, or the King would not, proceed to the solemnisation of this wedding, till these same were clearly purged, and the truth well and openly testified. Whereupon Dame Elizabeth Lucy was sent for. And albeit that she was by the King's mother and many other put in good comfort, to affirm that she was ensure unto the King: yet when she was solemnly sworn to say the truth, she confessed that they were never ensured. Howbeit she said his grace spake so loving words unto her, that she verily hoped he would have married her. And that if it had not been for such kind words, she would never have showed such kindness to him, to let him so kindly get her with child. This examination solemnly taken, when it was clearly perceived that there was none impediment, the King with great feast and honourable solemnity, married Dame Elisabeth Gray and her crowned Queen that was his enemy's wife, and many time had prayed full heartily for his loss. In which God loved her better, than to grant her boon.

But when the Earl of Warwick understood of this marriage, he took it so highly that his embassiate was deluded, that for very anger and disdain, he at his return assembled a great puissance against the King, and came so fast upon him ere he could be able to resist, that he was fain to void the realm and flee into Holland for succour.

Where he remained for the space of two years, leaving his new wife in Westminster in sanctuary, where she was delivered of Edward the prince, of whom we before have spoken. In which mean time the Earl of Warwick took out of prison and set up against Henry the sixth which was before by King Edward deposed and that much what by the power of the Earl of Warwick: which was a wise man and a courageous warrior, and of such strength, what for his lands his alliance and favour with all the people, that he made kings and put down kings almost at his pleasure, and not impossible to have attained it himself, if he had not reckoned it a greater thing to make a King than to be a King. But nothing lasteth always, for in conclusion King Edward returned, and with much less number than he had, at Barnet on the Easter day field, slew the Earl of Warwick with many other great estates of that party, and so stably attained the crown again, that he peaceably enjoyed it until his dying day: and in such plight left it, that it could not be lost, but by the discord of his very friends, or falsehood of his feigned friends.

I have rehearsed this business about this marriage somewhat the more at length, because it might thereby the better appear how slippery a ground the Protector builded his colour, by which he pretended King Edward's children to be bastards. But that invention simple as it was, it liked them to whom it sufficed to have somewhat to say, while they were sure to be compelled to no larger proof than themselves list to make.

Now then as I began to show you, it was by the Protector and his council concluded, that this doctor Shaw should in a sermon at Paul's Cross, signify to the people, that neither King Edward himself, nor the Duke of Clarence, were lawfully begotten, nor were not the very children of the Duke of York, but gotten unlawfully by other persons by the advoutry of the Duchess their mother. And that also Dame Elizabeth Lucy was verily the wife of King Edward, and so the prince and all his children bastards that were gotten upon the Queen. According to this devise, doctor Shaw the Sunday after at Paul's Cross in a great audience (as always assembled great number to his preaching) he took for his theme *Spuria vitulamina non agent radices altas.* That is to say bastard slips shall never take deep root. Thereupon when he had showed the great grace that God giveth and secretly infoundeth in the right generation after the laws of matrimony, then declared he that commonly those children lacked that grace, and for the punishment of their parents were for the most part unhappy, which were gotten in haste and specially in advoutry. Of which, though some by the ignorance of the world and the truth hid from knowledge inherited for the season other men's lands, yet God always so provideth, that it continueth not in their blood long, but the truth coming to light, the rightful inheritors be restored, and the bastard slip pulled up, ere it can be rooted deep. And when he had laid for the proof and confirmation of this sentence, certain ensamples taken out of the old testament and other ancient histories, then began he to descend into the praise of the Lord Richard late Duke of York, calling him father to the Lord Protector, and declared the title of his heirs unto the crown, to whom it was after the death of King Henry the sixth entailed by authority of parliament. Then showed he that his very right heir of his body lawfully begotten, was only the Lord Protector. For he declared then, that King Edward was never lawfully married, unto the Queen, but was before God, husband unto Dame Elizabeth Lucy, and so his children bastards. And besides that, neither King Edward himself, nor the Duke of Clarence among those that were secret in the household, were reckoned very surely for the children of the noble Duke, as those that by their favours more resembled other known men than him. From whose virtuous conditions, he said, that very noble prince, the special pattern of knightly prowess, as well in all princely behaviour as in the lineaments and favour of his visage, represented the very face of the noble Duke his father. This is quod he, the father's own figure, this is his own countenance, the very print of his visage, the sure undoubted image, the plain express likeness of that noble Duke.

Now was it before devised, that in the speaking of these words, the Protector should have come in among the people to the sermonward, to the end that those words meeting with his presence, might have been taken among the hearers, as though the Holy Ghost had put them in the preacher's mouth, and should have moved the people even there, to cry Richard King Richard, that it might have been after said, that he was specially chosen by God and in manner by miracle. But this device quailed either by the Protector's negligence, or the preacher's overmuch diligence. For while the Protector found by the way tarrying lest he should prevent those words, and the doctor fearing that he should come ere his sermon could come to those words hasted his matter thereto: he was come to them and past them and entered into other matters ere the Protector came. Whom when he beheld coming, he suddenly left the matter, with which he was in hand, and without any deduction thereunto, out of all order, and out of all frame, began to repeat those words again: this is the very noble prince, the special patron of knightly prowess, which as well in all princely behaviour, as in the lineaments and favour of his visage, representeth the very face of the noble Duke of York his father. This is the father's own figure, this his own countenance, the very print of his visage, the sure undoubted image, the plain express likeness of the noble Duke, whose remembrance can never die while he liveth. While these words were in speaking, the Protector accompanied with the Duke of Buckingham, went through the people into the place where the doctors commonly stand in the upper story, where he stood to hearken the sermon. But the people were so far from crying King Richard, that they stood as they had been turned into stones, for wonder of this shameful sermon. After which once ended, the preacher got him home and never after durst look out for shame, but keep him out of sight like an owl. And when he once asked one that had been his old friend, what the people talked of him, all were it that his own conscience well showed him that they talked no good, yet when the other answered him that there was in every man's mouth spoken of him much shame, it so struck him to the heart, that within few days after he withered and consumed away. Then on the Tuesday following this sermon, there came unto the guild hall in London the Duke of Buckingham, accompanied with divers Lords and knights, more than haply knew the message that they brought. And there in the east end of the hall where the Mayor keepeth the hustings, the Mayor and all the aldermen being assembled about him, all the commons of the city, gathered before them, after silence commanded upon great pain in the Protector's name: the Duke stood up, and (as he was neither unlearned, and of nature marvellously well spoken) he said unto the people with a clear and a loud voice in this manner of wise.

Friends, for the zeal and hearty favour that we bear you, we be come to break unto you, of a matter right great and weighty, and no less weighty, than pleasing to God and profitable to all the realm: nor to no part of the realm more profitable, than to you the citizens of this noble city. For why, that thing that we wot well ye have long time lacked and sore longed for, that ye would have given great good for, that ye would have gone far to fetch, that thing we be come hither to bring you, without your labour, pain, cost, adventure or jeopardy. What thing is that? certes the surety of your own bodies, the quiet of your wives and your daughters, the safeguard of your goods: of all which things in times past ye stood ever more in doubt. For who was there of you all, that would reckon himself Lord of his own good, among so many grins and traps as was set therefore, among so much pilling and polling, among so may taxes and tallages, of which there was never end, and often time no need: or if any were, it rather grew of riot and unreasonable waste, than any necessary or honourable charge. So that there was daily pilled from good men and honest, great substance of goods to be lashed out among unthrifts so farforth that fifteens sufficed not, nor any usual names of known taxes: but under an easy name of benevolence and good will, the commissioners so much of every man took, as no man would with his good will have given. As though the name of benevolence, had signified that every man should pay, not what himself of his good will list to grant, but what the King of his good will list to take. Which never asked little, but every thing was hawsed above the measure: amercements turned into fines, fines into ransoms, small trespass to misprision, misprision into treason. Whereof I think no man looketh that we should remember you of examples by name, as though Burdett were forgotten, that was for a word spoken in haste, cruelly beheaded, by the misconstruing of the laws of this realm for the prince's pleasure: with no less honour to Markham then Chief Justice, that left his office rather than he would assent to that judgement, than to the dishonesty of those, that either for fear or flattery gave that judgement. What, Coke your own worshipful neighbour alderman and Mayor of this noble city, who is of you either so negligent that he knoweth not, or so forgetful that he remembereth not, or so hard hearted that he pitieth not, that worshipful man's loss? What speak we of loss? his utter spoil and undeserved destruction, only for that it happed those to favour him, whom the prince favoured not. We need not I suppose to rehearse of these any more by name, sith there be I doubt not many here present, that either in themselves or their nigh friends, have known as well their goods as their persons greatly endangered, either by feigned quarrels, or small matters aggrieved with heinous names. And also there was no crime so great, of which there could lack a pretext. For sith the King preventing the time of his inheritance attained the crown by battle: it sufficed in a rich man for a pretext of treason, to have been of kindred or alliance near familiarity or leger acquaintance with any of those that were at any time the King's enemies, which was at one time and other, more than half the realm. Thus were neither your goods in surety and yet they brought your bodies in jeopardy beside the common adventure of open war, which albeit that it is ever the will and occasion of much mischief, yet is it never so mischievous, as where any people fall at distance among themselves, nor in none earthly nation so deadly and so pestilent, as when it happeneth among us and among us never so long continued dissension, nor so many battles in the season, nor so cruel and deadly fought, as was in the King's days that dead is God forgive it his soul. In whose time and by whose occasion, what about the getting of the garland, keeping it, losing and winning again, it hath cost more English blood than hath twice the winning of France.

In which inward war among ourselves, hath been so great effusion of the ancient noble blood of this realm, that scarcely the half remaineth, to the great enfeebling of this noble land, beside many a good town ransacked and spoiled, by them that have been going to the field or coming from thence. And peace long after not much surer than war. So that no time was there in which rich men for their money, and great men for their lands or some other for some fear or some displeasure were not out of peril. For whom trusted he that mistrusted his own brother? whom spared he that killed his own brother? or who could perfectly love him, if his own brother could not? what manner of folk he most favoured, we shall for his honour spare to speak of, howbeit this wot you well all, that whoso was best, bore always least rule, and more suit was in his days unto Shore's wife a vile and abominable strumpet, than to all the Lords in England, except unto those that made her their proctor which simple woman was well named and honest, till the King for his wanton lust and sinful affection bereft her from her husband a right honest substantial young man among you. And in that point which in good faith I am sorry to speak of, saving that it is in vain to keep in council that thing that all men know, the King's greedy appetite was insatiable, and everywhere over all the realm intolerable. For no woman was there anywhere young or old, rich or poor, whom he set his eye upon, in whom he anything liked either person or favour, speech, pace, or countenance, but without any fear of God, or respect of his honour, murmur or grudge of the world, he would importunely pursue his appetite, and have her, to the great destruction of many a good woman, and great dolour to their husband, and their other friends, which being honest people of themselves, so much regard the cleanness of their house, the chastity of their wives and their children, that them were lever to lose all that they have beside, than to have such a villainy done them. And all were it that with this and other importable dealing, the realm was in every part annoyed: yet specially ye here the citizens of this noble city, as well for that among you is most plenty of all such things as minister matter to such injuries, as for that you were nearest at hand, sith that near here about was commonly his most abiding. And yet be ye the people whom he had as singular cause well and kindly to entreat, as any part of his realm, not only for that the prince by this noble city, as his special chamber and the special well renowned city of his realm, much honourable fame receiveth among all other nations: but also for that ye not without your great caste and sundry perils and jeopardies in all his wars, bore ever your special favour to his part which your kind minds borne to the house of York, sith he hath nothing worthily acquitted, there is of that house that now by God's grace better shall, which thing to show you is the whole some and effect of this our present errand. It shall not I wot well need that I rehearse you again that ye have already hard, of him that can better tell it, and of whom I am sure ye will better believe it. And reason is that it so be. I am not so proud to look therefore, that ye should reckon my words of as great authority as the preachers of the word of God, namely a man so cunning and so wise that no man better wotteth what he should say, and thereto so good and virtuous that he would not say the thing which he wist he should not say, in the pulpit namely into which none honest man cometh to lie, which honourable preacher ye well remember substantially declared unto you at Paul's Cross on Sunday last past, the right and title that the most excellent Prince Richard Duke of Gloucester now Protector of this realm, hath unto the crown and kingdom of the same. For as that worshipful man groundly made open unto you, the children of King Edward the fourth were never lawfully begotten, forasmuch as the King (living his very wife Dame Elizabeth Lucy) was never lawfully married unto the Queen their mother, whose blood saving that he set voluptuous pleasure before his honour, was full unmeetly to be matched with his, and the mingling of whose bloods together, hath been the effusion of great part of the noble blood of this realm. Whereby it may well seem that marriage not well made, of which there is so much mischief grown. For lack of which lawful accoupling, and also of other things, which the said worshipful doctor rather signified than fully explained, and which things shall not be spoken for me as the thing wherein every man forebeareth to say that he knoweth in avoiding displeasure of my noble Lord Protector, bearing as nature requireth a filial reverence to the Duchess his mother, for these cause I say before remembered, that is to wit for lack of other issue lawfully coming of the late noble prince Richard Duke of York to whose royal blood the crown of England and of France, is by the high authority of parliament entailed, the right and title of the same, is by the just course of inheritance according to the common law of this land, devolute and come unto the most excellent prince the Lord Protector as to the very lawfully begotten son of the fore remembered noble Duke of York. Which thing well considered, and the great knightly prowess pondered, with manifold virtues which in his noble person singularly abound, the nobles and commons also of this realm, and specially of the north parts, not willing any bastard blood to have the rule of the land, nor the abusions before in the same used any longer to continue, have condescended and fully determined to make humble petition unto the most puissant prince, the Lord Protector: that it may like his grace at our humble request, to take upon him the guiding and governance of this realm, to the wealth and increase of the same, according to his very right and just title. Which thing I wot it well he will be loath to take upon him, as he whose wisdom well perceiveth the labour and study both of mind and of body that shall come therewith, to whomsoever so well occupy that room, as

I dare say he will if he take it. which room I warn you well is no child's office. And that the great wise man well perceived. When he said: *Vae regno cuius rex puer est.* Woe is that Realm, that hath a child to their King. Wherefore so much the more cause have we to thank God, that this noble personage which is so righteously entitled thereunto, is of so sad age, and thereto of so great wisdom joined with so great experience: which albeit he will be loath as I have said to take it upon him: yet shall he to our petition in that behalf the more graciously incline if ye the worshipful citizens of this the chief city of this realm, join with us the nobles in our said request. which for your own weal we doubt not but ye will, and natheless I heartily pray you so to do, whereby you shall do great profit to all this realm beside in choosing them so good a King, and unto yourself special commodity, to whom his majesty shall ever after bear so much the more tender favour, in how much he shall perceive you the more prone and benevolently minded toward his election. Wherein dear friends what mind you have, we require you plainly to show us. When the Duke had said, and looked that the people whom he hoped that the Mayor had framed before, should after this proposition made, have cried King Richard, King Richard: all was hushed and mute, and not one word answered thereunto. Wherewith the Duke was marvellously abashed, and taking the Mayor near to him, with the other that were about him privy to that matter, said unto them softly what meaneth this, that this people be so still. Sir quod the Mayor percase they perceive you not well. That shall we mend (quod he) if that will help. And by and by somewhat louder, he rehearsed them the same matter again in other order and other words, so well and ornately, and natheless so evidently and plain, with voice gesture and countenance so comely and so convenient, that every man much marvelled that heard him, and thought that they never had in their lives heard so evil a tale so well told. But were it for wonder or fear, or that each look that other should speak first: not one word was there answered of all the people that stood before, but all was as still as the midnight, not so much as rowning among them, by which they might seem to come what was best to do, when the Mayor saw this he with other partners of that council, drew about the Duke and said that the people had not been accustomed there to be spoken unto but by the Recorder, which is the mouth of the city, and haply to him they will answer.

With that the Recorder called Fitzwilliam a sad man and an honest, which was so new come into that office that he never had spoken to the people before, and loath was with that matter to begin, notwithstanding thereunto commanded by the Mayor, made rehearsal to the commons of that the Duke had twice rehearsed them himself. But the Recorder so tempered his tale, that he showed every thing as the Duke's words and no part of his own. But all this nothing no change made in the people which always after one, stood as they had been men amazed, whereupon the Duke rowned unto the Mayor and said: This is a marvellous obstinate silence, and therewith he turned unto the people again with these words: dear friends we come to move you to that thing which peradventure we not so greatly needed, but that the Lords of this realm and the commons of other parties, might have sufficed, saving that we such love bear you, and so much set by you, that we would not gladly do without you, that thing in which to be partners is your weal and honour which as it seemeth, either you see not or way not. Wherefore we require you give answer one or other, whether you be minded as all the nobles of the realm be, to have this noble Prince now Protector to be your King or not. At these words the people began to whisper among themselves secretly, that the voice was neither loud nor distinct, but as it were the sound of a swarm of bees, till at the last in the neither end of the hall, a bushment of the Duke's servants and Nashfield's and others belonging to the Protector, with some 'prentices and lads that thrust into the hall among the press, began suddenly at men's backs to cry out as loud as their throats would give: King Richard King Richard, and threw up their caps in token of joy. And they that stood before, cast back their heads marvelling thereof, but nothing they said. And when the Duke and the Mayor saw this manner, they wisely turned it to their purpose. And said it was a goodly cry and a joyful to hear, every man with one voice no man saying nay. Wherefore friends, quod the Duke, since that we perceive it is all your whole minds to have this nobleman for your King whereof we shall make his grace so effectual report, that we doubt not but it shall redound unto your great weal and commodity: we require ye that ye tomorrow go with us and we with you unto his noble grace, to make our humble request unto him in manner before remembered. And therewith the Lords came down, and the company dissolved and departed, the more part all sad, some with glad semblance that were not very merry, and some of those that came thither with the Duke, not able to dissemble their sorrow, were fain at his back to turn their face to the wall, while the dolour of their heart burst out at their eyes. Then on the morrow after, the Mayor with all the aldermen and chief commoners of the city in their best manner apparelled, assembling themselves together resorted unto Bainarde's Castle where the Protector lay. To which place repaired also according to their appointment the Duke of Buckingham, with divers noble men with him, beside many knights and other gentlemen. And thereupon the Duke sent word unto the Lord Protector, of the being there of a great and honourable company, to move a great matter unto his grace.

Whereupon the Protector made difficulty to come out unto them, but if he first knew some part of their errand, as though he doubted and partly distrusted the coming of such number unto him so suddenly, without any warning or knowledge, whither they came for good or harm, then the Duke when he had showed this unto the Mayor and other, that they might thereby see how little the Protector looked for this matter, they sent unto him by the messenger such loving message again, and therewith so humbly besought him to vouchsafe that they might resort to his presence, to purpose their intent, of which they would unto none other person any part disclose, that at the last he came forth of his chamber, and yet not down unto them, but stood above in a gallery over them, where they might see him and speak to him, as though he would not yet come to near them till he wist what they meant. And thereupon the Duke of Buckingham first made humble petition unto him, on the behalf of them all, that his grace would pardon them and licence them to purpose unto his grace the intent of their coming without his displeasure, without which pardon obtained, they durst not be bold to move him of that matter. In which albeit they meant as much honour to his grace as wealth to all the realm beside, yet were they not sure how his grace would take it, whom they would in no wise offend. Then the Protector as he was very gentle of himself, and also longed sore to wit what they meant, gave him leave to purpose what him liked, verily trusting for the good mind that he bore them all, none of them any thing would intend unto him ward, wherewith he ought to be grieved. When the Duke had this leave and pardon to speak, then waxed he bold to show him their intent and purpose, with all the causes moving them thereto as ye before have heard, and finally to beseech his grace, that it would like him of his accustomed goodness and zeal unto the realm, now with his eye of pity, to behold the long contrived distress and decay of the same and to set his gracious hands to the redress and amendment thereof, by taking upon him the crown and governance of this realm, according to his right and title lawfully descended unto him, and to the laud of God, profit of the land, and unto his grace so much the more honour and less pain, in that never prince reigned upon any people, that were so glad to live under his obeisance as the people of this realm under his. When the Protector had heard the proposition, he looked very strangely thereat, and answered: That all were it that he partly knew the things by them alleged to be true: yet such entire love he bore unto King Edward and his children, that so much more regarded his honour in other realms about, than the crown of any one, of which he was never desirous, that he could not find in his heart in this point to incline to their desire. For in all other nations where the truth were not well known, it should peradventure be thought, that it were his own ambitious mind and device, to depose the prince and take himself the crown. With which infamy he would not have his honour stained for any crown. In which he had ever perceived much more labour and pain, the pleasure to him that so would so use it, as he that would not were not worthy to have it. Not withstanding he not only pardoned them the motion that they made him, but also thanked them for the love and hearty favour they bore him, praying them for his sake to give and bear the same to the Prince, under whom he was and would be content to live, and with his labour and council as far as should like the King to use him, he would do his uttermost devoir to set the realm in good state. Which was already in this little while of his protectorship (the praise given to God) well begun, in that the malice of such as were before occasion of the contrary and of new intended to be, were now partly by good policy, partly more by God's special providence than man's provision repressed. Upon this answer given, the Duke by the Protector's licence, a little rowned, as well with other noble men about him as with the Mayor and Recorder of London. And after that upon like pardon desired and obtained, he showed aloud unto the Protector, that for a final conclusion, that the realm was appointed King Edward's line should not any longer reign upon them, both for that they had so far gone, that it was now no surety to retreat, as for that they thought it for the weal universal to take that way although they had not yet begun it. Wherefore if it would like his grace to take the crown upon him, they would humbly beseech him thereunto. If he would give them a resolute answer to the contrary, which they would be loath to hear, then must they needs seek and should not fail to find some other noble man that would. These words much moved the Protector, which else as every man may wit, would never of likelihood have inclined thereunto. But when he saw there was none other way, but that either he must take it or else he and his both go from it, he said unto the Lords and commons: Sith we perceive well that all the realm is so set, whereof we be very sorry that they will not suffer in any wise King Edward's line to govern them, whom no man earthly can govern again their wills, and we well also perceive, that no man is there, to whom the crown can by so just title appertain as to our self, as very right heir lawfully begotten of the body of our most dear father Richard late Duke of York, to which title is now joined your election, the nobles and commons of this realm, which we of all titles possible take for most effectual: we be content and agree favourably to incline to your petition and request, and according to the same, here we take upon us the royal estate, pre-eminence and Kingdom of the two noble realms, England and France, the one from this day forward by us and our heirs to rule, govern and defend, the other by God's grace and your good help to get again and subdue, and established for ever in due obedience unto this realm of England, the advancement whereof we never ask of God longer to live than we intend to procure. With this there was a great shout, crying Richard King Richard. And then the Lords went up to the King (for so was he from that time called) and the people departed, talking diversely of the matter every man as his fantasy gave him. But much they talked and marvelled of the manner of this dealing, that the matter was on both parts made so strange, as though neither had ever communed with other thereof before, when that themselves well wist there was no man so dull that heard them, but he perceived well enough, that all the matter was made between them. Howbeit some excused that again, and said all must be done in good order though. And men must sometime for the manner sake not be aknown what they know. For at the consecration of a bishop, every man wotteth well by the paying for his bulls, that he purposeth to be one, and though he pay for nothing else. And yet must he be twice asked whether he will be bishop or no, and he must twice say nay, and at the third time take it as compelled there unto by his own will. And in a stage play all the people know right well, that he that playeth the Sultan is percase a souter. Yet if one should can so little good, to show out of season what acquaintance he hath with him, and call him by his own name while he standeth in his majesty, one of his tormentors might hap to break his head, and worthy for marring of the play. And so they said that these matters be King's games, as it were stage plays, and for the more part played upon scaffolds. In which poor men be but the lookers-on. And they that wise be, will meddle no farther. For they that sometime step up and play with them, when they cannot play their parts, they disorder the play and do themselves no good.

The next day the Protector with a great train went to Westminster hall and there when he had placed himself in the court of the King's bench, declared to the audience, that he would take upon him the crown in that place there, where the King himself sitteth and ministreth the law: because he considered that it was the chiefest duty of a King to minister the laws. Then with as pleasant an oration as he could, he went about to win unto him, the nobles, the merchants, the artificers, and in conclusion all kind of men. But specially the lawyers of this realm. And finally to the intent that no man should hate him for fear, and that his deceitful clemency might get him the good will of the people, when he had declared the discommodity of discord, and the commodities of concord and unity, he made an open proclamation, that he did put out of his mind all enmities, and that he there did openly pardon all offences committed against him. And to the intent that he might show a proof thereof, he commanded that one Fogge whom he had long deadly hated, should be brought then before him. Who being brought out of the sanctuary by (for thither had he fled, for fear of him) in the sight of the people, he took him by the hand. which thing the common people rejoiced at and praised, but wise men took it for a vanity. In his return homeward, whom so ever he met he saluted. For a mind that knoweth itself guilty, is in a manner dejected to a servile flattery.

When he had begun his reign the twenty sixth day of June, after this mockish selection, than was he crowned the sixth day of July. And that solemnity was furnished for the most part, with the self-same provision that was appointed for the Coronation of his nephew.

Now fell there mischiefs thick. And as the thing evil gotten is never well kept: through all the time of his reign, never ceased there cruel death and slaughter, till his own destruction ended it. But as he finished his time with the best death, and the most righteous, that is to wit his own: so began he with the most piteous and wicked, I mean the lamentable murder of his innocent nephews, the young King and his tender brother. Whose death and final unfortune hath natheless so far come in question, that some remain yet in doubt, whither they were in his days destroyed or no. Not for that only that Perkin Warbeck, by many folk's malice, and more folk's folly, so long space abusing the world, was as well with princes as the poorer people, reputed and taken for the younger of those two, but for that also that all things were in late days so covertly demeaned, one thing pretended and another meant, that there was nothing so plain and openly proved, but that yet for the common custom of close and covert dealing, men had it ever inwardly suspect, as many well counterfeited jewels make the true mistrusted. Howbeit concerning that opinion, with the occasions moving either party, we shall have place more at large to entreat, if we hereafter happen to write the time of the late noble prince of famous memory King Henry the seventh, or percase that history of Perkin in any compendious process by itself. But in the mean time for this present matter, I shall rehearse you the dolorous end of those babes, not after every way that I have heard, but after that way that I have so heard by such men and by such means, as me thinketh it were hard but it should be true.

King Richard after his coronation, taking his way to Gloucester to visit in his new honour, the town of which he bore the name of his old, devised as he rode, to fulfil that thing which he before had intended. And forasmuch as his mind gave him, that his nephews living, men would not reckon that he could have right to the realm, he thought therefore without delay to rid them, as though the killing of his kinsmen, could amend his cause, and make him a kindly King. Whereupon he sent one John Green whom he specially trusted, unto Sir Robert Brakenbery constable of the Tower, with a letter and credence also, that the same Sir Robert should in any wise put the two children to death. This John Green did his errand unto Brakenbery kneeling before our Lady in the Tower, who plainly answered that he would never put them to death to die therefore, with which answer John Green returning recounted the same to King Richard at Warwick yet in his way. Wherewith he took such displeasure and thought, that the same night, he said unto a secret page of his: Ah whom shall a man trust? those that I have brought up myself, those that I had went would most surely serve me, even those fail me, and at my commandment will do nothing for me. Sir quod his page there lieth one on your pallet without, that I dare well say to do your grace pleasure, the thing were right hard that he would refuse, meaning by this Sir James Tyrell, which was a man of right goodly personage, and for nature's gifts, worthy to have served a much better prince, if he had well served God, and by grace obtained as much truth and good will as he had strength and wit. The man had an high heart, and sore longed upward, not rising yet so fast as he had hoped, being hindered and kept under by the means of Sir Richard Ratcliffe and Sir William Catesby, which longing for no more partners of the prince's favour, and namely not for him, whose pride they wist would bear no peer, kept him by secret drifts out of all secret trust. which thing this page well had marked and known. Wherefore this occasion offered, of very special friendship he took his time to put him forward, and by such wise do him good, that all the enemies he had except the devil, could never have done him so much hurt. For upon this page's words King Richard arose. (For this communication had he sitting at the draught, a convenient carpet for such a council) and came out in to the pallet chamber, on which he found in bed Sir James and Sir Thomas Tyrrel, of person like and brethren of blood, but nothing of kin in conditions. Then said the King merely to them: What sirs be ye in bed so soon, and calling up Sir James, broke to him secretly his mind in this mischievous matter. In which he found him nothing strange. Wherefore on the morrow he sent him to Brakenbury with a letter, by which he was commanded to deliver Sir James all the keys of the Tower for one night, to the end he might there accomplish the King's pleasure, in such thing as he had given him commandment. After which letter delivered and the keys received, Sir James appointed the night next ensuing to destroy them, devising before and preparing the means. The prince as soon as the Protector left that name and took himself as King, had it showed unto him, that he should not reign, but his uncle should have the crown. At which word the prince sore abashed, began to sigh and said: Alas I would my uncle would let me have my life yet, though I lose my Kingdome. Then he that told him the tale, used him with good words, and put him in the best comfort he could. But forthwith was the prince and his brother both shut up, and all other removed from them, only one called Black Will or William Slaughter except, set to serve them and see them sure. After which time the prince never tied his points, nor aught wrought of himself, but with that young babe his brother, lingered in thought and heaviness till this traitorous death, delivered them of that wretchedness. For Sir James Tyrrel devised that they should be murdered in their beds. To the execution whereof, he appointed Miles Forest one of the four that kept them, a fellow fleshed in murder before time. To him he joined one John Dighton his own horsekeeper, a big broad square strong knave. Then all the other being removed from them, this Miles Forest and John Dighton, about midnight (the silly children lying in their beds) came into the chamber, and suddenly lapped them up among the clothes so bewrapped them and entangled them keeping down by force the featherbed and pillows hard unto their mouths, that within a while smoored and stifled, their breath failing, they gave up to God their innocent souls into the joys of heaven, leaving to the tormentors their bodies dead in the bed.

Which after that the wretches perceived, first by the struggling with the pains of death, and after long lying still, to be thoroughly dead: they laid their bodies naked out upon the bed, and fetched Sir James to see them. Which upon the sight of them, caused those murderers to bury them at the stair foot, meetly deep in the ground under a great heap of stones. Than rode Sir James in great haste to King Richard, and showed him all the manner of the murder, who gave him great thanks, and as some say there made him knight. But he allowed not as I have heard, the burying in so vile a corner, saying that he would have them buried in a better place, because they were a King's sons. Whereupon they say that a priest of Sir Robert Brakenbury took up the bodies again, and secretly entered them in such place, as by the occasion of his death, which only knew it could never since come to light. Very truth is it and well known, that at such time as Sir James Tyrell was in the Tower, for treason committed against the most famous prince King Henry the seventh, both Dighton and he were examined, and confessed the murder in manner above written, but whither the bodies were removed they could nothing tell. And thus as I have learned of them that much knew and little cause had to lie, were these two noble princes, these innocent tender children, born of most royal blood, brought up in great wealth, likely long to live to reign and rule in the realm, by traitorous tyranny taken, deprived of their estate, shortly shut up in prison, and privily saline and murdered, their bodies cast God wot where by the cruel ambition of their unnatural uncle and his dispiteous tormentors. Which things on every part well pondered: God never gave this world a more notable example, neither in what unsurety standeth this worldly well, or what mischief worketh the proud enterprise of an high heart, or finally what wretched end ensueth such dispiteous cruelty. For first to begin with the ministers, Miles Forest at Saint Martin's piecemeal rotted away. Dighton in deed walketh on alive in good possibility to be hanged ere he die. But Sir James Tyrrel died at Tower Hill, beheaded for treason. King Richard himself as ye shall hereafter hear, slain in the field, hacked and hewed of his enemies' hands , harried on horseback dead, his hair in despite torn and tugged like a cur dog. And the mischief that he took, within less than three years of the mischief that he did. And yet all the mean time spent in much pain and trouble outward, much fear anguish and sorrow within. For I have heard by credible report of such as were secret with his chamberers, that after this abominable deed done, he never had quiet in his mind, he never thought himself sure.

Where he went abroad, his eyes whirled about, his body privily fenced, his hand ever on his dagger, his countenance and manner like one always ready to strike again, he took ill rest a-nights, lay long waking and musing, sore wearied with care and watch, rather slumbered than slept, troubled with fearful dreams, suddenly sometime started up, leapt out of his bed and run about the chamber, so was his restless heart continually tossed and tumbled with the tedious impression and stormy remembrance of his abominable deed. Now had he outward no long time in rest. For hereupon soon after began the conspiracy or rather good confederation, between the Duke of Buckingham and many other gentlemen against him. The occasion whereupon the King and the Duke fell out, is of divers folk divers wise pretended. This Duke as I have for certain been informed, as soon as the Duke of Gloucester upon the death of King Edward came to York, and there had solemn funeral service for King Edward, sent thither in the most secret wise he could, one Pearsall his trusty servant, who came in to John Ward a chamberer of like secret trust with the Duke of Gloucester, desiring that in the most close and covert manner, he might be admitted to the presence and speech of his master. And the Duke of Gloucester advertised of his desire, caused him in the dead of the night after all other folk avoided, to be brought unto him in his secret chamber, where Pearsall after his master's recommendation showed him, that he had secretly sent him to show him, that in this new world he would take such part as he would, and wait upon him with a thousand good fellows if need were. The messenger sent back with thanks, and some secret instruction of the Protector's mind: yet met him again with farther message from the Duke his master, within a few days after at Nottingham: whither the Protector from York with many gentlemen of the North country to the number of six hundred horses, was come on his way to London-ward. And after secret meeting and communication had, eftsoon, departed. Whereupon at Northampton the Duke met with the Protector himself, with three hundred horses and from thence still continued with, partner of all his devices, till that after his coronation they departed as it seemed very great friends at Gloucester. From whence as soon as the Duke came home, he so lightly turned from him and so highly conspired against him, that a man would marvel whereof the change grew. And surely the occasion of their variance is of divers men diversely reported. Some have I heard say, that the Duke a little before the coronation among other things, required of the Protector the Duke of Hereford's lands, to which he pretended himself just inheritor. And forasmuch as the title which he claimed by inheritance, was somewhat interlaced with the title to the crown by the line of King Henry before deprived: the Protector conceived such indignation, that he rejected the Duke's request with many spiteful and minatory words. which so wounded his heart with hatred and mistrust, that he never after could endure to look aright on King Richard, but ever feared his own life, so farforth that when the Protector rode through London toward his coronation, he feigned himself sick, because he would not ride with him. And the other taking it in evil part, sent him word to rise, and come ride or he would make him be carried. Whereupon he rode on with evil will, and that notwithstanding on the morrow rose from the feast feigning himself sick, and King Richard said it was done in hatred and despite of him. And they say that ever after continually each of them lived in such hatred and distrust of other, that the Duke verily looked to have been murdered at Gloucester. From which nathless he in fair manner departed. But surely some right secret at the days deny this: and many right wise men, think it unlikely, (the deep dissimuling nature of those both men considered, and what need in that green world the Protector had of the Duke, and in what peril the Duke stood if he fell once in suspicion of the tyrant) that either the Protector would give the Duke occasion of displeasure, or the Duke the Protector occasion of mistrust. And utterly men think, that if King Richard had any such opinion conceived: he would never have suffered him to escape his hands. Very truth it is, the Duke was an high minded man, and evil could bear the glory of another, so that I have heard of some that said they saw it, that the Duke at such time as the crown was first set upon the Protector's head, his eye could not abide the sight thereof, but wried his head another way. But men say that he was of truth not well at ease, and that both to King Richard well known, and not ill taken, nor any demand of the Duke's uncourteously rejected, but he both with great gifts and high behests, in most loving trusty manner departed at Gloucester. But soon after his coming home to Brecknock, having there in his custody by the commandment of King Richard, doctor Morton bishop of Ely, who as ye before heard was taken in the council at the Tower, waxed with him familiar. Whose wisdom abused his pride to his own deliverance and the Duke's destruction. The bishop was a man of great natural wit, very well learned, and honourable in behaviour, lacking no wise ways to win favour. He had been fast upon the part of King Henry while that part was in wealth, and nathless left it not nor forsook it in woe, but fled the realm with the Queen and the prince, while King Edward had the King in prison, never came home but to the field. After which lost, and that part utterly subdued, the other for his fast faith and wisdom, not only was content to receive him, but also wooed him to come and had him from thenceforth both in secret trust and very special favour, which he nothing deceived. For he being as ye have heard after King Edward's death, first taken by the tyrant for his truth to the King, found the mean to set this Duke in his top, joined gentlemen together in aid of King Henry, devising first the marriage between him and King Edward's daughter, by which his faith declared and good service to both his masters at once, with infinite benefit to the realm, by the conjunction of those two bloods in one, whose several titles had long enquieted the land, he fled the realm, went to Rome, never minding more to meddle with the world till the noble prince King Henry the seventh got him home again, made him archbishop of Canterbury and Chancellor of England whereunto the Pope joined the honour of Cardinal. Thus living many days in as much honour as one man might well wish, ended them so godly, that his death with God's mercy well changed his life. This man therefore as I was about to tell you, by the long and often alternate proof, as well of prosperity as adverse fortune, had gotten by great experience the very mother and masters of wisdom, a deep insight in politic worldly drifts. Whereby perceiving now this Duke glad to come with him, fed him with fair words and many pleasant praises. And perceiving by the process of their communications, the Duke's pride now and then baulk out a little braid of envy toward the glory of the King, and thereby feeling him ethe to fall out if the matter were well handled: he craftily sought the ways to prick him forward taking always the occasion of his coming and so keeping himself close within his bonds, that he rather seemed him to follow him than to lead him. For when the Duke first began to praise and boast the King, and show how much profit the realm should take by his reign: my Lord Morton answered: surely my Lord folly were it for me to lie, for if I would swear the contrary, your lordship would not I ween believe, but that if the world would have gone as I would have wished, King Henry's son had had the crown and not King Edward. But after that God had ordered him to lose it, and King Edward to reign, I was never so mad, that I would with a dead man strive against the quick. So was I to King Edward faithful chaplain, and glad would have been that his child had succeeded him. Howbeit if the secret judgement of God have otherwise provided: I purpose not to spurn against a prick, nor labour to set up that God pulleth down. And as for the late Protector and now King. And even there he left, saying that he had already meddled to much with the world, and would from that day meddle with his book and his beads and no farther. Then longed the Duke sore to hear what he would have said, because he ended with the King and there so suddenly stopped, and exhorted him so familiarly between them twain, to be so bold to say whatsoever he thought, whereof he faithfully promised there should never come hurt and peradventure more good than he would ween, and that himself intended to use his faithful secret advice and counsel which he said was the only cause for which he procured of the King to have him in his custody where he might reckon himself at home, and else had he been put in the hands of them, with whom he should not have found the like favour. The bishop right humbly thanked him and said, in good faith my Lord I love not much to talk much of princes, as thing not all out of peril, though the word be without fault forasmuch as it shall not be taken as the party meant it, but as it pleaseth the prince to consider it. And ever I think on Æsop's tale, that where the lion had proclaimed that on pain of death there should none horned beast abide in that wood, one that had in his forehead a bunch of flesh, fled away a great pace. The fox that saw him run so fast, asked him whither he made all that haste. And he answered, in faith I neither wot nor reck, so I were once hence because of this proclamation made of horned beasts. What fool quod the fox thou mayest abide well enough, the lion meant not by thee, for it is none horn that is in thine head. No marry quod he that wot I well enough. But what and he call it an horn, where am I then? The Duke laughed merely at the tale, and said, my Lord I warrant you, neither the lion nor the boar shall pique any matter at any thing here spoken, for it shall never come near their ear. In good faith Sir said the bishop if it did, the thing that I was about to say, taken as well as afore God I meant it, could deserve but thank. And yet taken as I ween it would, might happen to turn me to little good and you to less. Then longed the Duke yet much more to wit what it was. Whereupon the bishop said: in good faith my Lord, as for the late Protector, sith he is now King in possession, I purpose not to dispute his title. But for the weal of this realm, whereof his grace hath now the governance, and whereof I am myself one poor member, I was about to wish, that to those good abilities whereof he hath already right many, little needing my praise: it might yet have pleased God for the better store, to have given him some of such other excellent virtues meet for the rule of a realm, as our Lord hath planted in the person of your grace.

The History of King Richard the Third (Continued) From the edition of Hardyng's Chronicle, printed by Richard Grafton, 1543

By which words the Duke perceiving that the Bishop bore unto him his good heart and favour, mistrusted not to enter more plain communication with him so far, that at the last the Bishop declared himself to be one of them that would gladly help that Richard, who then usurped the crown, might be deposed, if he had known how it might conveniently be brought to pass that such a person as had true title of inheritance unto the same, might be restored thereunto. Upon this the said Duke, knowing the Bishop to be a man of prudence and fidelity, opened to him all his whole heart and intent, saying, my Lord, I have devised the way of the blood of both of King Edward and of King Henry the sixth, that is left, being coupled by marriage and affinity may be restored unto the crown, being by just and true title due unto them both, (for King Richard he called not the brother of King Edward the fourth, but his enemy and mortal foe). The way that the Duke had devised was this, that they should with all speed and celerity find means to send for Henry Earl of Richmond (whom the rumour went immediately upon knowledge of King Edward's death to have been delivered out of prison with Francis Duke of Brittany) and the same Henry to help with all their power and strength, so that the said Henry would first, by his faithful oath, promise that immediately upon the obtaining the crown, he would marry and take to wife Elizabeth, the elder daughter of Edward the fourth. The Bishop of Ely right well allowed both the device and purpose of the Duke, and also the manner and way how the matter should be brought to effect, and found means that Reynold Bray, servant with Margaret mother of the said Henry then married to Thomas Stanley, came to the Duke into Wales, and the Duke's mind thoroughly perceived and known, with great speed returned to the said Margaret, advertising the same of all things which was between the Duke and him concerning as well the common weal of the realm, as also the advancement of her and her blood that had been debated.

Now it came so to pass that the Duke of Buckingham and the Lady Margaret mother to the said Henry, had been in communication of the same matter before, and that the said Lady Margaret had devised the same mean and way for the deposition of King Richard and bringing in of Henry her son, the which the Duke now broke unto the Bishop of Ely, whereupon there rested no more, forasmuch as she perceived the Duke now willing to prosecute and further the said device, but that she should find the means that this matter might be broken unto Queen Elizabeth, the wife of King Edward the fourth then being in sanctuary. And here upon which she caused one Lewes that was her physician, in his own name and as though it came of himself, to break this matter unto the Queen, saying that if she would consent and agree thereunto, a mean might be found how to restore again the blood of King Edward and King Henry the sixth unto the crown, and to be avenged of King Richard for the murder of King Edward's children, and then declared that there was beyond the sea Henry Earl of Richmond, which was of the blood of King Henry the sixth, whom if she would be content that he marry might Elizabeth her eldest daughter, there should of his side be made right many friends, and she for her part might help in like manner, whereby no doubt it should come to pass that he should possess the crown by most rightful inheritance. Which matter, when she heard it, it liked her exceedingly well, insomuch as she counselled the said physician to break the same unto his mistress the Lady Margaret and know her mind therein, promising upon her word that she would make all the friends of King Edward to take part with the said Henry if he would be sworn that when he came to the possession of the crown, he would immediately take in marriage Elizabeth her eldest daughter, or else if she lived not at that time, that then he would take Cicely her youngest daughter.

Whereupon the said Lewes returned unto the Lady Margaret his mistress declaring unto her the whole mind and intent of the Queen. So that then it was shortly agreed between these two women, that with all speed this matter should be set forward, insomuch that the Lady Margaret broke this matter unto Reynold Bray, willing him to move and set forward the same with all such as he should perceive either able to do good or willing thereunto. Then had the Queen devised that one Christopher (whom the aforesaid Lewes the physician had promoted into her service) should be sent into Brittany to Henry to give him knowledge of their minds here, and that he should prepare and appoint himself ready and to come into Wales, where he should find aid and help enough ready to receive him.

But then shortly after came unto her knowledge that the Duke of Buckingham had of himself afore intended the same matter, whereupon she thought it should be meet to send some messenger of more reputation and credit than was this Christopher, and so kept him at home, and then sent Hugh Conway with a great sum of money, willing him to declare unto Henry all things, and that he should haste him to come and to land in Wales as is aforesaid. And after him one Richard Guilford out of Kent sent one Thomas Ramney with the same message, the which two messengers came in manner both at one time into Brittany to the Earl Henry, and declared unto him all their commissions. The which message, when Henry had received and thoroughly heard, it rejoiced his heart, and he gave thanks unto God, full purposing with all convenient speed to take his journey towards England, desiring the aid and help of the Duke of Brittany, with promise of thankful recompense when God should send him to come to his right. The Duke of Brittany notwithstanding that he had not long after been required by Thomas Hutton purposely sent to him from King Richard in message with money eftsoons to imprison the said Henry Earl of Richmond and there continually to keep and hold the same from coming into England, yet with all gladness and favour inclined to the desire of Henry and aided him as he might with men, money, ships and other necessaries. But Henry while he might accordingly appoint and furnish himself, remained in Brittany sending afore the said Hugh Conway and Thomas Ramney, which two were to him very true and faithful, to bear tidings into England unto his friends of his coming, as also for seeing such dangers as might befall, and avoiding such traps and snares as by Richard the third and his complices might be set for him and for all his other company that he should bring with him.

In the meantime, the friends of Henry with all care, study, and diligence wrought all things unto their purpose belonging. And though all this were as secretly wrought and conveyed as among so great a number was possible to be, yet privy knowledge thereof came to the ears of King Richard, who although he were at the first hearing much abashed, yet thought best to dissemble the matter as though he had no knowledge thereof, while might secretly gather unto him power and strength, and by secret spial among the people get more perfect knowledge of the whole matters and chief authors and contrivers of the same. And because he knew the chief and principal of them, as unto whom his own conscience knew that he had given most just causes of enmity, he thought it necessary first of all to dispatch the same Duke out of the way. Wherefore, unto the Duke he addressed letters enforced and replenished with all humanity, friendship, familiarity and sweetness of words, willing and desiring the same to come unto him with all convenient speed. And further gave in commandment to the messenger that carried the letters that he should in his behalf make many high and gay promises unto the Duke and by all gentle means persuade the same to come unto him. But the Duke, mistrusting the fair words and promises so suddenly offered of him, of whose wily crafts and means he knew sundry examples afore practiced, desired the King his pardon, excusing himself that he was diseased and sick, and that he might be ascertained, that if it possible were for him to come, he would not absent himself from his grace. This excuse the King would not admit, but eftsoons directed unto the Duke other letters of a more rough sort, not without menacing and threatening unless he would according to his duty repair unto him at his calling, whereunto the Duke plainly made answer that he would not come to him whom he knew to be his enemy. And immediately the Duke prepared himself to make war against him, and persuaded all his complices and partakers of his intent with all possible expedition, some in one place and some in another, to stir against King Richard. And by this means and manner, at one time and hour, Thomas Marquis of Dorchester raised an army within the County of York, being himself late come forth of sanctuary, and by the means and help of Thomas Rowell, preserved and saved from peril of death. And in Devonshire, Edward Courtnay with his brother Peter, Bishop of Exeter, raised in like manner an army, and in Kent, Richard Guilford accompanied with certain other gentleman raised up the people, as is aforesaid, and all this was done in manner in one moment. But the King, who had in the meantime gathered together great power and strength, thinking it not to be best by pursuing everyone of his enemies to disparkle his company in small flocks, determined to let pass all the others, and with all his whole puissance to set upon the chief head, that is to say the Duke of Buckingham: so taking his journey from London he went towards Salisbury to the intent that he might set upon the said Duke, in case he might have perfect knowledge that the same lay in any field embattled. And now was the King within two days journey of Salisbury when the Duke attempted to meet him, which Duke being accompanied with great strength of Welshmen, whom he had enforced thereunto and coerced, more by lordly commandment than by liberal wages and hire, which thing indeed was the cause that they fell from him and forsook him. Wherefore he being suddenly forsaken of his men, was of necessity constrained to flee, in which doing, as a man cast in sudden and therefore great fear, of this his sudden change of fortune, and by reason of the same fear not knowing where to be come, nor where to hide his head, nor what in such case best to do, he secretly conveyed himself into the house of Humphrey Bannister, in whom he had conceived a sure hope and confidence to find faithful and trusty unto him, because the same had been and then was his servant, intending therefore to remain in secret until he might either raise a new army, or else by some means convey himself into Brittany to Henry Earl of Richmond. But as soon as the others, which had attempted the same enterprise against the King, acknowledge that the Duke was forsaken of his company and fled and could not be found, they being stricken with sudden fear, made every man for himself such shift as he might, and being in utter despair of their health and life, either got them to sanctuaries or desert places, or else assayed to escape oversea, and many of them indeed arrived safely in Brittany, among whom were these whose names ensue. Peter Courtney Bishop of Exeter with his brother Edward Earl of Devonshire, Thomas Marquis of Dorchester with his son Thomas being a very young child, John Bourshere, John Welsh, Edward Woodville a stout man of arms and brother to Elizabeth the Queen, Robert Willoughby, Giles Daubeney, Thomas Arundel, John Cheney with his two brethren, William Berkeley, William Brandon with Thomas his brother, Richard Edgecome, and all these for the most part knights. Also John Halliwell, Edward Pointz an excellent good captain and Christopher Urswick, but John Morton the Bishop of Ely at the same self time together with sundry of the nobles and gentlemen sailed into Flanders.

But Richard the king, who was now come to Salisbury and had gotten perfect knowledge that all these parties sought to flee the realm, with all diligence and haste that might be, sent to all the port towns there about, to make sure stay that none of them might pass untaken, and made proclamation that whosoever should bring him knowledge, where the Duke of Buckingham were to be had, should have for his reward, if he were a bondman, his freedom, and if he were free, his pardon and besides that, a thousand pounds of money.

Furthermore because he understood by Thomas Hutton newly returned out of Brittany, of whom afore is mentioned, that Francis Duke of Brittany would not only not hold Henry Earl of Richmond in prison for his sake, but also was ready to help the same Henry with men, money and ships in all that he might against him, he set divers and sundry ships in places convenient by all the sea coasts to Brittany-ward that if Henry should come that way, he might either be taken before his arrival, or else might be kept from landing in any coast of England. And furthermore in every coast and corner of the realm, laid wonderful wait and watch to take partly any other of his enemies, and especially the said Duke of Buckingham. Whereupon the said Humphrey Bannister (were it for meed or for losing his life and goods,) disclosed him unto the King's inquisitors, who immediately took him, and forthwith all brought him to Salisbury where King Richard was. The Duke being diligently examined uttered without any manner refusal or sticking, all such things as he knew, trusting that for his plain confession he should have liberty to speak with the King, which he made most instant and humble petition that he might do. But as soon as he had confessed his offence towards King Richard, he was out of hand beheaded. And this death of the Duke received at the hands of King Richard whom he had before holpen in his affairs and purposes beyond all God's forebode.

While these things were in hand in England, Henry Earl of Richmond made ready his host strength to the number of five thousand Bretons and fifteen ships, the day appointed of his departure being now come, which was the twelfth day of the month of October, in the year of our Lord God a thousand four hundred fourscore and four, and the second year of the reign of King Richard and having a fair wind, hoisted up the sails and set forward, but towards the night came such a tempest that they were dispersed from one another some into Brittany and some into Normandy. But the ship in which Henry was, with one other ship, tossed all the night with the waves of the sea and tempest, when the morning came, it waxed somewhat calm and fair weather, and they were come toward the south part of England, by a haven or port called Poole, where the said Henry saw all the shores and banks set full of harnessed men, which were soldiers appointed there to wait by King Richard, as we have said before, for the coming and landing of the Earl. While Henry there abode he gave commandment, that no man should land before the coming of the other ships. And in the meantime that he waited for them, he sent a little boat with a few in it aland to know what they were that stood on the shore, his friends or enemies. To whom those soldiers, being before taught but they should say, answered that they were the friends of Henry, and were appointed by the Duke of Buckingham there to abide his coming and to conduct him to those castles and holds, where his tents pavilions and artillery for the war lay, and where remained for him a great power that intended now with all speed to set upon King Richard while he was now fled for fear and clean without provision, and therefore besought him to come aland.

Henry suspecting this to be but fraud, after that he saw none of his ships appeared, hoisted up the sails, having a marvellous good wind, even appointed him of God to deliver him from that great jeopardy, and sailed back again into Normandy. And after his landing there, he and his company after their labours, arrested them for the space of three days, determining to go from thence afoot into Brittany, and in the meanwhile sent messengers unto Charles the French King, the son of Louis that a little before departed, beseeching him of liberty and licence to pass through Normandy into Brittany. The young King Charles, being sorry for his fortune, was not only ready and well pleased to grant his passage, but also sent him money to help him further in his journey. But Henry before that he knew the King his mind (not doubting of his great humanity and gentleness), had sent away his ships towards Brittany, and had set himself forwards in his journey, but made no great haste till the messengers returned, which great gentleness when he received from the King, rejoiced his heart and with a lusty stomach and good hope set forward into Brittany, there to take farther counsel of his affairs.

And when he was in Brittany, he received from his friends out of England knowledge that the Duke of Buckingham was beheaded, and that the Marquis of Dorchester with a great number of the noblemen of England had been there a little before to seek him, and that they were now in Vannes a city in Brittany. The which things being known to the Earl, he on the one part to greatly lament the death and evil chance of his chief and principal friend, but yet on the other part he greatly rejoiced in that he had so many and noble men to take his part in the battle. And therefore conceiving a good hope and opinion that his purpose should well frame and come to pass, determined with himself with all expedition to set forward, and thereupon went to a place in Brittany called Redon, and from thence sent the Marquis with all the other noblemen that they should come to him. Then when they heard that Henry was safe returned into Brittany rejoiced not a little, for they had thought he had landed in England, and so fallen into the hands of King Richard, and they made not a little haste till they were come unto him. The which when they met after great joy and gladness as well of their part of his, they began to talk of their prepensed matters, and now was Christmas come, on the which day they all together assembled in the church and there swore faith and truth one to another. And Henry swore first, promising that as soon as he should possess the crown of England, that he would marry Elizabeth the daughter of King Edward the fourth and afterwards they swore fealty and homage unto him, even as though he had already been King, and so from that time forth did take him, promising him that they would spend both their lives and goods with him, and that Richard should no longer reign over them. When this was done, Henry declared all these things to the Duke of Brittany, praying and desiring him now of help, and that he would aid him with a greater number of men, and also to lend him a friendly and honest sum of money, that he might now recover his right and inheritance of the crown of England, unto the which he was called and desired by all the Lords and nobility of the realm, and which (God willing) he was most assured to possess, and after his possession he would most faithfully restore the same again. The Duke promised him aid, upon the trust whereof he began to make ready his ships that they might with all expedition be ready to sail, but no time should be lost. In the which time King Richard was again returned to London, and had taken divers of them that were of this conspiracy that is to say George Brown, Roger Clifford, Thomas Salinger, knights. Also Thomas Ram, Robert Clifford and divers others whom he caused to be put to death.

After this he called a Parliament, wherein was decreed that all the lords that were fled out of the land should be reputed and taken as enemies to the realm, and all their lands and goods to be forfeit and confiscate. And not content with that prey, which was no small thing, he he called also a great tax and sum of money to be levied of the people. For the large gifts and liberality that he first used, to buy the favours and friendships of many, had now brought him in need. But nothing was more like than that Thomas Stanley should have been reputed and taken for one of those enemies, because of the working of Margaret his wife, which was mother unto Henry Earl of Richmond, the which was noted for the chief head and worker of this conspiracy. But forasmuch as it was thought that was to small purpose that women could do, Thomas being nothing faulty was delivered and commanded that he should not suffer Margaret his wife to have any servants about her, neither that she should not go abroad, but to be shut up and that from thenceforth she should send no message neither to her son nor to any of her other friends, whereby any hurt might be wrought against the King, the which commandment was accomplished. And by the authority of the same Parliament a peace was concluded with the Scots, which a little before had skirmished with the borderers. Which thing brought to pass, the King supposed all conspiracy to be clean avoided, for as much of the Duke with other of his company were put to death, and also certain other banished. Yet for all this, King Richard was daily vexed and troubled, partly mistrusting his own strength, and partly fearing the coming of Henry with his company, so that he lived but in a miserable case. And because that he would not so continue any longer, he determined with himself to put away the cause of this his fear and business, either by policy or else by strength. And after that he had thus purposed with himself, he thought nothing better than to tempt the Duke of Brittany yet once again either with money, prayer or some other special reward, because that he had in keeping the Earl Henry, and most chiefly, because he knew that it was only he that might deliver him from all his trouble by delivering or imprisoning the said Henry. Wherefore incontinently he sent unto the Duke certain ambassadors the which should promise unto him, beside other great rewards that they brought with them, to give him the yearly all the revenues of all the lands of Henry and of all the other lords there being with him, if he would after the receipt of the ambassadors put them in prison. The ambassadors, being departed and come where the Duke lay, could not have communication with him, forasmuch as by extreme sickness his wits were feeble and weak. Wherefore one Peter Landose his treasurer a man both of pregnant wit and great authority, took the matter in hand. For which cause he was afterward hated of all the lords of Brittany. With this Peter the English ambassadors had communication, and declaring to him the King his message desired him instantly, forasmuch as they knew that he might bring their purpose to pass, that he would grant unto King Richard his request, and he should have the yearly revenues of all the lands of the said lords. Peter, considering that he was greatly hated of the lords of his own nation, thought that if he might bring to pass through King Richard to have all these great possessions and the yearly revenues, he should then be able to match with them well enough and not to care a rush for them, whereupon he answered the ambassadors that he would do that King Richard did desire, if he broke not promise with him. And this did he not for any hatred that he bore unto Henry, for he hated him not, for not long before he saved his life where the Earl Henry was in great jeopardy. But such was the good fortune of England, that this crafty compact took no place, for while the letters and messengers ran between Peter and King Richard, John the Bishop of Ely being then in Flanders was certified by a priest, which came out of England whose name was Christopher Urswick, of all the whole circumstance of this device and purpose. Whereupon with all speed the said Bishop caused the said priest the same day to carry knowledge thereof into Brittany to Henry Earl of Richmond, willing him with all the other noblemen to dispatch themselves with all possible haste into France. Henry was then in Vannes, when he heard of this fraud without tarriance sent Christopher unto Charles the French King desiring license that Henry with the other noblemen might safely come into France, which thing being soon obtained, the messenger returned with speed to his Lord and Prince.

Then the Earl Henry setting all his business in as good stay and order as he might, talked little and made few a counsel thereof, and for the more expedition, he caused the Earl of Pembroke secretly to cause all the noblemen to take their horses, dissembling to ride unto the

Duke of Brittany: but when they came to the uttermost parts thereof, they should forsake the way that led them toward the Duke, and to make into France with all that ever they might. Then they, doing in everything as they were bidden, lost no time but so sped them that shortly they obtained and got into the County of Anjou. Henry then within two days following, being then still at Vannes took four or five of his servants with him and feigned as though he would have ridden thereby to visit a friend of his; and forasmuch as there were many English men left there in the town, no man suspected anything, but after that he had kept the right way for the space of five miles, he forsook that and turned straight into a wood that was thereby, and took upon him his servants apparel, and put his apparel upon his servant and so took but one of them with him, on whom he waited as though he had been the servant and the other the master. And with all convenient and speedy haste so set forth upon their journey that no time was lost, and obeyed no more tarriance by the way, than only the baiting of their horses, so that shortly he recovered the coasts of Anjou, where all his other company was.

But within four days after that the Earl was thus escaped Peter received from King Richard the confirmation of the grant and promises made for the betraying of Henry and the other nobles. Wherefore the said Peter sent out after him horses and men with such expedition and speed to have taken him, that scarcely the Earl was entered France one hour but they were at his heels. The English then then being above the number of three hundred at Vannes, hearing that the Earl and all the nobles were fled so suddenly and without any of their knowledge, were astonied and in manner despaired of their lives.

But it happened contrary to their expectation for the Duke of Brittany, taking the matter so unkindly that Henry should be so used with him that for fear he should be compelled to flee his land, was not a little vexed with Peter, to whom (although that he was ignorant of the fraud and craft that had been wrought by him) yet he laid the whole fault in him, and therefore called unto him Edward Poynings and Edward Woodville, delivering unto them the foresaid money that Henry before had desired the Duke to lend him toward the charge of his journey, and commanded them to convey and conduct all the Englishman his servants unto him paying their expenses, and to deliver the said sum of money unto the Earl. When the Earl saw his men, and heard the comfortable news, he not a little rejoiced, desiring the messengers that returned to show unto the Duke, that he trusted ere long time to show himself not to be unthankful for this great kindness that he now showed unto him. And within a few days after, the Earl went unto Charles the French King, to whom after he had rendered thanks for the great benefits and kindness that he had received of him, the cause of his coming first declared, then he besought him of his help and aid, which should be an immortal benefit to him and his lords, of whom generally he was called unto the kingdom, forasmuch as they so abhorred the tyranny of King Richard. Charles promised him help and bade him to be of good cheer and to take no care, for he would gladly declare unto him his benevolence. And the same time Charles removed and took with him Henry and all the other noblemen.

While Henry remained there, John Earl of Oxford (of whom is before spoken) which was put in prison by King Edward the fourth in the Castle of Hammes with also James Blunt captain of that castle, and John Fortescue knight, porter of the town of Calais, came unto him. But James the captain, because he left his wife in the castle, did furnish the same with a good garrison of men before his departure.

Henry, when he saw the Earl, was out of measure glad that so noble a man and of great experience in battle, and so valiant and hardy a knight, whom he had thought to be most fateful and sure, for so much as he had, in the time of King Edward the fourth, continual battle with him in defending of King Henry the sixth, thought that now he was so well appointed that he could not desire to be better, and therefore communicated to him all his whole affairs, to be ordered and ruled only by him. Not long after Charles the French King removed again to Paris, whom Henry followed, and there again moved and besought the King as he had most favourably and kindly entertained him all this time, not only in words but also in deeds, that it would likewise please him yet so much further to extend his favour and benevolence unto him, that now he would aid and help them forward in his journey, that not only he, but also all the Lords and nobility of England might justly have cause to knowledge and confess that by the mean of his favour and goodness they were restored again to the possession of their inheritances, which without him they could not well bring to pass.

In the meanwhile, his fortune was such, that many English men came over daily out of England unto him, and many which were then in Paris, among whom were divers students that fell unto his part both more and less, and specially there was one, whose name was Richard Foxe a priest, being a man of a singular good wit and learning, whom Henry straightaway retained and committed all his secrets unto him and whom also afterwards he promoted to many high promotions, and at the last he made him Bishop of Winchester.

King Richard then, hearing of all this conspiracy and of the great aid that daily went over to Henry, thought yet for all this, that if he might bring to pass that Henry should not couple in marriage with the blood of King Edward, that then he should do well enough with him and keep him from the possession of the crown. Then devised he with himself all the ways and means that might be how to bring this to pass. And first he thought it to be best with fair and large promises to attempt the Queen, whose favour obtained, he doubted not but shortly to find the means to have both her daughters out of her hands into his own, and then rested nothing but if he himself might find the means afterward to marry one of the same daughters, whereby he thought he should make all sure and safe to the utter disappointing of Henry. Whereupon he sent unto the Queen, then being in the sanctuary, divers and sundry messengers that should excuse and purge him of his fact afore done towards her, setting forth the matter with pleasant words and high promises both to her and also her son Thomas Lord Marquis of Dorset, of all things that could be desired. These messengers being men of gravity, handled the Queen so craftily that anon she began to be allured and to hearken unto them favourably, so that in conclusion she promised to be obedient to the King in his requests (forgetting the injuries he had done to her before, and on the other part not remembering the promise that she made to Margaret, Henry's mother). And first she delivered both her daughters into the hands of King Richard, then after she said privily for the Lord Marquis her son being then at Paris with Henry (as you have heard) willing him to forsake Henry with whom he was, speedily to return into England, for all things was pardoned and forgiven, and she again in favour and friendship of the King, and it should be highly for his advancement and honour.

King Richard (when Queen Elizabeth was thus brought into a fool's paradise) after he had received all his brother's daughters from the sanctuary into his palace, thought their now remained nothing to be done, but only the casting away and destroying of his own wife, which thing he had wholly purposed and decreed within himself. And there was nothing that feared him so much from this most cruel and detestable murder as the losing of the good opinion that he thought the people had conceived of him, far as ye have heard before, he feigned himself to be a good man and thought the people had esteemed him even so. Notwithstanding shortly after, his foresaid ungracious purpose overcame all this honest fear. And first of all, he found himself grieved with the barrenness of his wife, that she was unfruitful and brought forth no children, complaining thereof very grievously unto the nobles of this realm, and chiefly above other unto Thomas Rotherham, then Archbishop of York (whom he had delivered a little before out of prison), the which Bishop did gather of this, that the Queen should be rid out of the way, ere it were long after (such experience had he of King Richard's complexion, who had practised many like things not long before) and at the same time also he made divers of his secret friends privy of the same his conjecture.

After this he caused a rumour to run among the common people (but he would not have the author known) that the Queen was dead, to the intent that she hearing this marvellous rumour, should take so grievous a conceit that anon after she should fall into some great disease, so that he would assay that way, in case it should chance her afterward to be sick, dead, or otherwise murdered, that then the people right imputed her death unto the thought she took, or else to sickness. But when the Queen heard of so horrible rumour of her death sprung abroad among the common people, she suspected the matter and supposed the world to be at an end with her, and incontinently, she went to the King with a lamentable countenance, and with weeping tears asked him, whether she had done anything whereby he might judge her worthy to suffer death. The King made answer with a smiling and dissimuling countenance and with flattering words, bidding her to be of good comfort and to pluck up her heart for there was no such thing toward her that he knew. But howsoever it fortuned, either by sorrow or else by poisoning, within a few days after the Queen was dead and afterward was buried in the Abbey of Westminster. This is the same Anne, one of Richard the Earl of Warwick's daughters, which once was contacted to Prince Edward, King Henry the sixth his son.

The King being thus delivered of his wife fantasied apace Lady Elizabeth his niece, desiring in any wise to marry with her, but because that all men, yea and the maiden herself, abhorred this unlawful desire, as a thing most detestable, he determined with himself to make no great haste in the matter, chiefly for that he was in a peck of troubles, fearing lest that of the noblemen some would forsake him and run unto Henry his part, the other at the least would favour the secret conspiracy made again him, so that of his end there was almost no doubt. Also the more part of the common people were in so great despair, that many of them had rather to be accounted of the number of his enemies, than to put themselves in jeopardy both of loss of body and goods in taking of his part.

And amongst those noblemen whom he feared, first was Thomas Stanley and William his brother, Gilbert Talbot, and other great number, of whose purpose though King Richard was ignorant, nevertheless he trusted not one of them, and least of all Thomas Stanley, because he had married Henry's mother, as it may well appear by this that followeth. For when the said, this would have departed from the court until his own mansion for his recreation (as he said) the truth was, because he would be in a readiness to receive Henry and aid him at his coming into the realm. But the kingdom did let him, and would not suffer him to depart, until such time as he had left in the court behind him George Strange, his son and heir, for a pledge. And while King Richard was thus wrapped in fear, and care of the tumult that was to come, lo, even then tidings came that Henry was entered into the land, and that the Castle of Hammes was prepared to receive Henry by the means of the Earl of Oxford which then was fled, with James Blunt keeper of the castle, unto Henry.

Then King Richard, thinking at the beginning to stay all this matter, sent forth with all haste the greater part that were then at Calais to recover the said castle again. Those that were in the castle, when they saw their adversaries make towards them, speedily they armed themselves to defence, and in all haste sent messengers to Henry, desiring him of aid. Henry forthwith sent the Earl of Oxford with a chosen sort of men to assist them, and at their first coming they laid siege not far from the castle. And while King Richard's men turned back having an eye towards them, Thomas Brandon, with thirty valiant men of the other side, got over a water into the castle, to strength them that were within. Then they that were within laid hard to their charge that were without; on the other side, the Earl of Oxford so valiantly assailed them of the back side that they were glad to make proclamatiunto them that were within, that if they would be content to give over the castle, they should have free liberty to depart with all that ever they had. The Earl of Oxford hearing this, which came only to save his friends from hurt, and namely James Blunt's wife, was contented with this condition and departed in safeguard with all his friends, returning back to Henry, which was in Paris. After this, King Richard was informed that the French king was weary of Henry and his company, and would do nothing for him, whereby Henry was now not able in manner to help himself, so that it was not possible that he should prevail or go forward in the enterprise that he thought to have taken in hand against King Richard. King Richard being brought thus into a fool's paradise, thought himself to be out of all fear, and that there was no cause why he should, being so sure, once to wake out of his sleep or trouble himself any further, and therefore called back his Navy of ships that then was ready upon the sea, which was fully furnished to have scoured the seas. But yet for the more surety, lest he should be suddenly oppressed, he gave commandment to the great men dwelling by the seaside (and especially the Welshmen) to watch night and day, lest his adversaries should have any opportunity to enter into the land. As the fashion is in time of war that those that dwelt by the sea side should make beacons in the highest places there about, which might be seen afar off, so that when it should chance their enemies to arrive toward the land, by and by they should fire their beacons and raise the country, to the intent that quickly from place to place they might be ascertained of all the whole matter, and also to arm themselves speedily against their enemies.

And so to come to our purpose again, King Richard through the aforesaid tidings, began to be more careless and reckless, as who say, he had no power to withstand of the destiny that hung over his head. Such is the provident justice of God, that a man doth least know, provide and beware when the vengeance of God is even at hand for his offences. And to go forth, at that time when Henry the Earl of Richmond remained in France entreating and suing for aid and help of the Frenchmen, many of the chief noblemen, which had the realm in governance (because of the young age of Charles the King), fell somewhat at dissension, of the which variance, Louis the Prince of Orleans was the chief and head, which because he had married Joan the King's sister looked to have been chief Governor of all the realm. By the which means it came to pass, that one man had the principal governance of the realm. And therefore Henry the Earl was constrained to sue unto all the nobles severally one after another desiring and praying them of aid and help in his purpose, and thus the matter was prolonged. In the meantime Thomas the Marquis of Dorset (of whom we spoke afore) was privily sent for to come home by his mother, partly mistrusting that Henry should not prevail, and partly for the great and large promises that King Richard had made to her for him before. Which letters when the said Marquis had received, he believing all things that his mother wrote unto him, and also thinking that Henry should never prevail, and that the Frenchmen did but mock and delay with him, he suddenly in the night-time conveyed himself out of Paris and with great speed made towards Flanders. The which thing when the Earl and other of the English Lords heard of, they were sore astonied and amazed, and with all speed purchased of Charles the King a licence and commandment that the Marquis might be stayed, wheresoever he were found within the Dominion of France, chiefly for that he was secret of their counsel and knew all their purpose. The commandment was quickly obtained and posts made forth every way, among whom one Humphrey Cheney playing the part of a good bloodhound so truly smelled out and followed the trace, that by and by he found out and took the Marquis, and so handled and persuaded him with gentle and good words, that shortly after he was content to return.

Then Henry, being delivered of this chance, thought it best to prolong the matter no further lest he should lose both the present opportunity and also weary his friends that looked for him in England. Wherefore he made haste and set forward with a small army obtained of the French king, of whom he also borrowed some money, and some of other his friends, for the which he left the Marquis and John

Burchere behind for a pledge. And so setting forward came to Rouen, and while he tarried there and prepared shipping at the haven of Seine, tidings came to him that King Richard's wife was dead, and purposed to marry with the lady Elizabeth, King Edward's eldest daughter being his neice, and that he had married Cicely her sister to a man's son of the land far underneath her degree. At the which thing, Henry was saw amazed and troubled, thinking that by this means all his purpose was dashed, for that there was no other way for him to come to the kingdom but only by the marriage of one of King Edward's daughters. And by this means also he feared lest his friends in England would shrink from him for lack of an honest title. But after they had consulted upon the matter, they thought it best to tarry a little to prove if they might get more help and make more friends. And among all other, they thought it best to adjoin the Lord Herbert unto them, which was a man of great power in Wales, and that should be brought to pass by this means, for that the Lord Herbert had a sister marriable, whom Henry would be content to marry if he would take their part. And to bring all this matter to pass messages were sent to Henry the Earl of Northumberland, which had married the other sister, so that he should bring this matter about, but the ways were so beset that the messengers could not come to him.

And in the mean the season came very good tidings from John ap Morgan, a temporal lawyer, which signified unto them that Sir Rhys ap Thomas, a noble and valiant man, and John Savage favoured his part earnestly, and also Sir Reynold Bray had prepared a great sum of money to wage battle on his part and to help him, and therefore he would they should make haste with all that ever they could, and make toward Wales.

Then Henry speedily prepared himself because he would linger his friends no longer. And after that he had made his prayer unto Almighty God that he might have good success in his journey, only with two thousand men and a few ships in the kalends of August he sailed from the haven of Seine, and the seventh day after which was the twenty second day of August, he arrived in Wales about sunset and landed at Milford Haven, and in the part which is called the Dale, where he was very joyfully received. Here he had contrary tidings brought to that he heard in Normandy afore, that Sir Rhys ap Thomas and John Savage, with all that ever they could make, were of King Richard's part.

Notwithstanding, they had such tidings sent them from the men of Pembroke by a valiant gentleman, whose name was Arnold Butler, that it rejoiced all their hearts, which was, that if all former offences might be remitted, they would be in a readiness to stick unto their own Gaspard the Earl. Then Henry's company by this means being increased, departed from Hereford five mile toward Cardigan, and then while he refreshed his men, suddenly came rumour unto him that the Lord Herbert, which dwelled at Carmarthen, was nigh at hand with a great army of men. At the which rumour there was a great stir amongst them, every man took himself to his weapon and made themselves ready if need were to fight, and a little while they were all afraid, till such time as Henry had sent out horsemen to try the truth, which when they came again, declared that all things was quiet and that there was no such thing. But most of all Master Griffiths, a very noble man, did comfort them and gladden their hearts which although before he had joined himself to the Lord Herbert, at that very time he cleaved to Henry with such company as he had, though they were but few, and the same time came John ap Morgan unto him. Henry went still forward and tarried almost in no place, because he would make sure work and the better speed, he invaded such places afore that they were armed against him, the which places he beat down with very little strength. But afterward, having knowledge by his spies that the Lord Herbert and Sir Rhys were in a readiness to give him battle, he determined to set upon them, and either to put them to flight or else to make them swear homage and fealty unto him, and to take them with him in his host against King Richard. And because he would ascertain his friends in England how all the matter went forward with him, he sent his most trusty friends to the lady Margaret his mother, to Stanley, to Talbot, and two other of his most special friends with certain commandments. The effect of the commandments were, that he intended with the help of his friends to pass over Severn and by Shrewsbury to make toward London.

Therefore he desired them with those that were of their counsel, in time and place convenient, to meet him. So the messenger is going forth with these commissions, Henry went forward toward the

Shrewsbury, and in the way met with Sir Rhys ap Thomas with a great number of men which came unto him and was of his part. For two days afore Henry promised him to be chief ruler of all Wales as soon as he came to the crown (if he would come to him) which afterward he gave to him indeed. In the meantime the messengers executing the message diligently returned back again with large rewards of them to whom they were sent, and came to Henry the same day he entered into Shrewsbury and showed how all his friends were in a readiness to do the uttermost that lay in them. This tidings put Henry in such great hope, that he went forth with a courage and came to the town of Newport and there set up his tents upon a little hill, and there lay all night. At night came to him Sir Gilbert Talbot with above two hundred men. After that they went forth to Stafford and while they were there, William Stanley came to him with a few after him, and when he had talked a little with him, returned back again to his host which he had prepared. From thence he went to Lichfield and that night lay without the town, but in the morning betime he entered into the city and was received honourably. A day or two afore, Thomas Stanley was there with five thousand men armed, which, when he knew of Henry's coming, forthwith went afore to a village called Adderstone there to tarry till Henry came. This he did to avoid suspicion, being afraid lest King Richard knowing his intent would have put his sunto death, which, as I told you before, was left with him as a pledge for his father. But King Richard in the meantime, which then was at Nottingham, hearing that Henry with a few more of banished men was entered into Wales, so lightly regarded to the matter, that he thought it was not much to be passed upon, for that he came in with so few in number, and that the Lord Herbert and Sir Rhys, which were rulers of all Wales, would either kill him, or else take him and bring him alive. But afterward, when he remembered himself that oftentimes a small matter in battle, if it be not looked unto betimes, would make at the last a great stir, he thought it best to remedy the matter betimes and commanded Henry the Earl of Northumberland with other of the nobles of the realm (whom he thought had set more by him than by their own goods) to raise up an army and to come to him with speed. Also he sent divers messengers with letters to Robert Brackenbury, keeper of the Tower of London, commanding him to come unto him in all haste, and to bring with him, as fellows in battle, Thomas Bircher,

Walter Hungerford and divers other knights, whom he did not a little suspect.

In this time it was showed that Henry was come to Shrewsbury without any hurt. With the which tidings, the King began to rage and make exclamation against them, that contrary to their faiths they had utterly deceived him, and then he began to mistrust all men, and wist not whom he might trust, so that he thought it best to set forth himself against his adversaries. And forthwith he sent out spies to know which way Henry did take. They when they had done their diligence returned back again and showed him how that Henry was come to Lichfield. The which thing after he knew, because now there was a great number of soldiers come together, by and by his men set in array, he commanded them forward, and to go for and for together, and by that way which they kept they heard say, their enemies were coming. The suspect persons he put in the midst, he himself with those he trusted came behind, with wings of horsemen running on every side. And thus keeping their order, about sunset came unto Leicester.

When Henry in the mean season had removed from Lichfield unto the next village called Tamworth, in the midway he met with Walter Hungerford, Thomas Bircher and many other more, which had promised to aid him afore. And for because they perceived that they were suspected of King Richard, and lest they should be brought violently unto him, being their enemy, they forsook Robert Brackenbury their captain and in the night-time stole privily away and went to Henry. Unto whom there chanced by the way that was worthy to be marked, which was that Henry, although he was a man of noble courage and also his company did daily increase, yet for all that stood in great fear because he was uncertain of Thomas Stanley which, as I told you before, for the fear of putting his sons to death, inclined as yet unto no part, and that the matter was not so slender of King Richard, as report was made to him of his friends.

Wherefore, as all afraid without a cause, he took only twenty men with him, and started his journey as a man in despair and half musing with himself what was best to be done. And to aggravate the matter, tidings was brought him that King Richard was coming near to meet him with a great and huge host of men. And while he thus lingered for fear behind, his host came afore to the town of Tamworth, and because it was then dark night, he lost both his company and also his way, then wandering from place to place, at last came to a little village three mile from his host, being full of fear, and lest he should fall into the danger of the scoutwatch he durst not ask a question on any man, and partly for the fear that was present, and partly for that was to come delayed there that night and took this for a sign or a prognostication of some great plague that was to come, and the other part of his host was no less abashed seeing his absence for that time. When in the morning Henry came to them in the light of the day he excused the matter that he was not absent because he had lost his way, but rather of purpose, because he would commune with his privy friends which would not be seen in the day. And after that he went privily to Adderstone where Thomas Stanley and William his brother did dwell. Here Henry, Thomas, and William met and took other by the hand with loving salutations and were glad one of another. Then after they counselled together of their meeting with King Richard whom they perceived not then to be far from them. That day withdrew toward night, in the evening John Savage, Brittany Sanford, Simon Digby with many other had forsaken King Richard and came to Henry with a great power of men, which power and strength set Henry aloft again. In the mean season King Richard which purposed to go through thick and thin in this matter came to Bosworth a little beyond Leicester where the place of battle should be (as a man would say the high justice of God, which could not be avoided, hanging over his head, and called him to a place where he should suffer worthy punishment for his detestable offences) and there he set up his tents and rested that night. Afore he went to bed, he made an oration to his company with great vehemence, persuading and exhorting them manfully to fight. And afterward, as it was said, he had a horrible dream in his sleep, seeming that he saw horrible devils appear unto him and pulling and hauling of him that he could take no rest, which vision filled full of fear and also of heavy care when he waked. For by and by after, being sore grieved in his mind, he did prognosticate of this dream the evil luck and heavy chance that after came to him, and he came not with so cheerful countenance unto his company as he was wont to do. Then, lest they should think that he had this heaviness for the fear of his enemies, he stood up and rehearsed unto them all his dream. But I think that this was not a dream, but rather his conscience pricked with the sharp sting of his mischievous offences, which although they do not prick alway, yet most commonly they will bite most toward the latter day, representing unto us not only themselves, but also the terrible punishment that is ordained for the same, as the sight of the devil tearing and hauling us, so that thereby (if we have grace) we may take an occasiunto be penitent, or else for lack of the same die in desperation. Now to come to my purpose again, the next day after, King Richard having all things in readiness went forth with the army out of his tents, and began to set his men in array; first the forward set forth a marvellous length both of horsemen and also of footmen, a very terrible company to them that should see them afar off; and in the foremost part of all he ordered the bowmen as a strong fortress for them that came after, and over this John the Duke of Norfolk was head captain. After him followed the King with a mighty sort of men.

And in this while, Henry, being departed from the communication of his friends, without any tarrying pitched his tents near his enemies and lay there all night and commanded his men to be in a readiness. In the morning he sent also to Thomas Stanley, being then in the midst betwixt both hosts, that he should come near with his army. He sent word again that he should set his men in an order till he came; with the which answer, otherwise than he had thought or than the matter did require, he was not a little abashed and stood as it were in doubt. Yet for all that he tarried not, but with all speed set his men in an order, the forward was but slender, because his number was but few, the archers were set in the foremost part. Over them John the Earl of Oxford was head captain. In the right wing he set Gilbert Talbot. In the left he put John Savage. And he himself with the help of Thomas Stanley followed with one company of horsemen and a few footmen, for all his his whole company were scant five thousand besides both the Stanleys with their company, of the which William Stanley had three thousand. The King his army was double to all this. And so when both armies were all in a readiness and began for to come within the sight of other, they bragged forth themselves of both parties, looking only for the sign and token of striking together. Betwixt both hosts, there was a morass which Henry left on his right hand purposely as a defence of his men, he found the means also to have the bright sun on his back, that it might dazzle the eyes of his enemies.

But the King, when he saw Henry pass over the morass, commanded his men with all violence to set upon them. They by and by with a sudden clamour let arrows fly at them. On the other side they paid them home manfully again with the same. But when they came near together they laid on valiantly with swords. The Earl of Oxford fearing lest in the meantime King Richard's multitude should have compassed in his men, which were but a few, he commanded them by fives they should not move forward past ten foot, the which commandment known, they knit themselves together and ceased not in fighting: their adversaries being afraid suspected some craft or guile and began to break off, and many of the same part were not much grieved therewith, because they were as glad the King should be lost as saved, and therefore they fought with less courage. Then the Earl of Oxford, with his men thick together, struck on more freshlier. The other of the other part did likewise the same. And while the first wards of the battle had fought so manfully, Richard perceived by his spies Henry afar off with a few company of armed men. Afterward coming near, Richard knew him by signs and tokens, then being inflamed with an anger, furiously struck the horse with the spurs and ran out of the one side of the host, and like a lion ran at him. On the other side Henry, perceiving him coming, was very desirous to meet him. Richard at the first setting forth killed divers that stood before him, and again he threw down Henry's banner and William Brandon the bearer also, he ran at Cheney, a man of great might, which came for to meet him, and with great violence overthrew him to the ground, and thus he made himself a way through them for to come to Henry. But Henry kept better tack with him than his men would have thought, which then was almost in despair of the victory. And even at that time lo there came William Stanley to aid them with three thousand men, and even at the very same time the residue of King Richard's men were put to flight. Then Richard fighting alone in the midst of all his enemies was overthrown and slain. In the meantime the Earl of Oxford in the forward, after he had fought manfully a little while, put the residue to flight of whom he slew a great number. But a great number more, which followed Richard more for fear than for love, held their hands from fighting and went away without hurt for that they looked not for his safeguard, but rather for his destruction. There were slain in this conflict not many more than one thousand of the which these were noblemen: John Duke of

Norfolk, Walter Ferris, Robert Brackenbury, Richard Radcliffe and many other more. And within two days after, William Catesby lawyer with certain other of his fellows was put to death at Leicester, and among those that ran away was Francis Lovell, Humphrey Stafford, with Thomas his brother, and many other more that ran into sanctuary at Colchester in Essex. There was of the captives a great number, because that when King Richard was slain, every man cast down his weapon and yielded himself to Henry, of the which the more part would have done so at the beginning, if it had not been for fear of King Richard's spies, which then wandered in every place. And amongst these, the nobles were the Earl of Northumberland, the Earl of Surrey, of the which the Earl of Surrey was put in prison, the other as a friend was received into favour. Henry at that field lost not above a hundred men amongst whom the chief was William Brandon which bore Henry's banner. This battle was fought on the twenty seventh day of the month of August, in the year of our Lord one thousand four hundred and eighty-six. The conflict endured more than two hours. Richard might (as the fame went) have saved himself if he would have fled away, for those that were about him, when they saw his men from the beginning fight but faintly and that some were run away to the other part, suspected treason and willed him to fly, and when the matter was manifest that all hope of victory was passed, they brought him a swift horse. He putting aside all hope and trust that was in flying, made (as it was said) this answer, that this day he would have either an end of battle or else of his life, such was his great audacity and manfulness which because he did see certainly that in this day he should obtain the kingdom quietly all days of his life or else lose both forever, he entered in amongst them, as it was declared before, intending utterly either to lose all or else to win all. And so the wretch died, having the end that all such were wont to have, which in the stead of law, honesty and all godliness follow their own appetite, villainy and all wickedness. And plainly this is an example which cannot be expressed, to fear them which will not suffer one hour to be otherwise spent than in cruelty, mischief and all devilish fashions. Henry when he had thus obtained the victory he fell down on his knees and, with many prayers and thanks, referred all to the goodness of God. Then after he stood up being wonderfully replenished with joy, and went up upon a little hill and there gave great commendations to his soldiers, commanding them that were hurt to be healed and the dead to be buried; afterward he gave mortal thanks to his noble captains promising them that he would never forget their benefit. The multitude in the meantime with one voice and one mind proclaimed him King. When Thomas Stanley saw that, he took King Richard his crown which was found amongst the spoil, and by and by put it upon Henry's head as though he had been then created King by the election of the people as it was wont to be in the old time, and this was the first token of his felicity. After this King Henry with his company and carriage went to Leicester toward night to bed, where, after he had refreshed his company well for the space of two days, that they might the better go toward London, King Richard's body was brought naked over a horse back, the head and the arms hanging on the one side and the legs on the other, and carried into the Greyfriars of Leicester, and surely it was but a miserable sight look upon, yet it was good enough considering his wretched living, and there without any solemnity was buried two days after. He reigned two years two months and one day. He was but of a small stature having but a deformed body, the one shoulder was higher than the other, he had a short face and a cruel look which did betoken malice, guile and deceit. And while he did muse upon any thing standing, he would bite his underlip continually, whereby a man might perceive his cruel nature within his wretched body strived and chafed always within himself, also the dagger which he bore about him, he would always be chopping of it in and out. He had a sharp and pregnant wit, subtle, and to dissimule and feign very meet. He had also a proud and cruel mind, which never went from him to the hour of his death, which he had rather suffer by the cruel sword, though all his company did forsake him, than by shameful flight he would favour his life, which after might fortune by sickness or other condign punishment shortly to perish.

The End of The History of King Richard III.